an eye for an eye

an eye for an eye

Bandula Chandraratna

Best wishes

Bandula Chandraratna

Weidenfeld & Nicolson

London

A PHOENIX HOUSE BOOK

First published in Great Britain in 2001 by Phoenix House

A CIP catalogue record for this book is available
from the British Library.

ISBN 1 86159187 X

Typeset by Selwood Systems, Midsomer Norton
Printed by Butler & Tanner Ltd, Frome and London

Phoenix House

Weidenfeld and Nicolson
The Orion Publishing Group Ltd
Orion House
5 Upper Saint Martin's Lane
London, WC2H 9EA

It is always a mystery to me that men
feel themselves honoured by the humiliation
of their fellow human beings.

Mahatma Gandhi

To my dearest teacher
Mrs Nalini Chitra Jayasuriya –
the lady who taught me how to write.

Chapter 1

It was Friday, the Middle Eastern Sunday. The city was quiet, with only a few vehicles on the road. The grocery shop outside the hospital gate was shut, its metal shutters pulled down. The women's dress shop next to it and Dr Abdullah's stationery shop were shut too. The nurses' home next door was quiet, washing lines laden with colourful clothes curtaining the balconies. The man at the hospital switchboard on the ground floor of the staff residential building was still sleeping on the mat on the floor near the switchboard.

Nimal was shaving with his electric razor, standing near the bedroom window of his apartment on the second floor of the staff residential building. He could see the waste ground below where his beloved soft-top Toyota Land Cruiser and his American friend David's red Nissan Patrol four-wheel drive were parked. The crossroads to the left, at the corner of the building, was the scene of many vehicle crashes. The locals would drive on the wings of the wind across the junction, blowing their horns and hoping for the best. Sometimes the crashes involved ten to fifteen cars, with Buicks,

Pontiacs, Cadillacs crushing the flimsy Toyotas, Mazdas and Nissans. Nimal's old car was smashed at the crossroads in a pile-up that involved a local and an Egyptian schoolteacher. Its right side was completely caved in, and the local was refusing to share the costs: 'fifty-fifty', as the policeman at the central police station ordered. It was always fifty-fifty, and it did not matter whose fault it was. The local was willing to go to jail instead. The next two days were spent going to the car repair *souk*, drinking tea and Arabic coffee with repair shop owners and the local and the Egyptian teacher, and haggling over the cost of repairs. Finally, when a deal was made, hands shaken, cheeks kissed, lips dabbed, bear-hugs exchanged, Nimal took a taxi and returned to the hospital.

When Nimal's car came back from repairs you could still see the road through the floor, and the steering wheel was at an angle. So Nimal took it to the car *souk* with two of his Scottish friends who were giving him moral support, and part-exchanged it for his beloved Land Cruiser. They put humps on the road at the crossroads to stop the kamikaze drivers killing each other, but still you saw big American cars jump-jetting over the humps.

Nimal finished shaving and cleaned his razor. He could see a local man in a white *thorbe* and red chequered *gutra* crouching on the waste ground next to an abandoned dust-covered cerulean Volkswagen beetle whose wheels had sunk in the red sand. From the direction of the airport he could hear the thundering take-off noise of the refuelling aircraft for the American-owned AWACS spy plane which was patrolling the borders. Now Nimal could see the black aircraft over the apartment blocks, flying towards the east with four long trails of grey smoke curving upwards behind it.

Nimal's two daughters were sleeping in the next room, and his wife was busy in the kitchen. While Nimal was taking a shower the telephone rang. Padmawathi banged on the door. Nimal walked across the steam-filled bathroom and opened the door slightly. His wife handed him a cordless telephone.

'Hello.'

'Sabah il-khayr, Nimal.'

'Morning, David. How are you?'

'Fine. You OK?'

'Could be better.'

'How long will you be?'

'About an hour.'

'Don't tell the wife where you are going.'

'No need to. Don't tell yours either.'

'Nope. You're dragging me to this, you know.'

'I don't think so, David. You don't have to come. I am going anyway.'

'I'm coming, my boy, but it's on your head.'

'See you in about an hour, David.'

'Sure thing.'

Nimal got dressed and Padmawathi made him breakfast: egg and a beef rasher with toast and marmalade.

He listened to the BBC World Service on his short-wave radio while eating it. After a mug of black coffee he lit a King Edward cigar, sat back in an easy chair and put his feet up on one of the dining chairs. The ash at the tip of the cigar was growing and he did not want to break it. He wondered how long it would hold. A good cigar, he was once told by someone, could hold the ash until the end. He was enjoying the taste of the tobacco on his tongue and the smoke in his mouth and nostrils. The smoke was curling away towards the extractor fan above the glass door to the balcony.

On a Thanksgiving Day in the middle of the holy month of Ramadan, David had cooked his turkey on his balcony, in a barbecue with a lid. Instead of burning charcoal he used squashed newspaper balls. The smoke was immense and it permeated all the way down the road towards the newly opened Movenpick restaurant, and spread over the east side of the building. All the air-conditioning units on that side sucked the smoke into the apartments.

Dr Mohammad Salah, the Deputy Director of the hospital, was fasting and resting peacefully with his family in his apartment on the third floor. He came running out in his white *thorbe* without his *gutra* on his bald head, coughing and sneezing and waving his hands as if to push the smoke away, trying to shout but without the words coming out. His wife and children came running out after him. He was very angry.

4

The nurses on the top floor came out of their apartments, but they were locked up there and could not come down to any lower floors. David had to pour water on to the barbecue to stop the smoke, and the turkey was too big for the oven. David was very apologetic to Dr Salah and to all his neighbours. He narrowly escaped being reported to the religious police for cooking during Ramadan. Fortunately for David, the Scots were on the ground floor and were not affected.

The doorbell rang. Nimal carefully broke the length of ash in the ashtray and pressed the stub hard on the glass to extinguish it. He put his eye to the spy hole in the door. He could see David standing outside, wearing an Arabic *thorbe* and holding a plastic water bottle. He opened the door.

'Ke fel Hal?' David asked, in his strong American accent.

'Al Hamdulillah, shukran, David, and you?'

'Tayyib.'

'Please sit down. Why only half a bottle of water?'

'Not water, sadeki,' David said, sitting down on the settee.

'Sadeki? You must be joking. That's alcohol. It's like vodka. If you get caught we're both finished.'

'Don't worry. This looks like water, and I bet you we'll need it afterwards, where you're taking us. Sadeki means "my friend", my friend.'

'Where did you get it?'

'I have my supplies, boy. It's good stuff.'

'Would you like a coffee?'

'You don't know how to make coffee.'

'I'll try my best. I will ask Padma to make it.'

'Black then. No sugar. We've got to go soon.'

Nimal walked into the kitchen and asked his wife to make two cups of coffee, then came back to the sitting room.

'Did you hear about the aircraft fire?'

'The whole country knows about that, boy.'

'I telephoned Al Bentley. The Yank who works at the airport. You know Al, don't you?'

'I've heard of him. Never met him. He works for one of the aircraft maintenance companies, doesn't he?'

'That's him. He was on duty when it happened.'

'I heard some Pakistanis were trying to cook curries using a gas burner.'

'That's rubbish! The aircraft was about to land. It was fine all the way from Karachi. Then the fire started when they were approaching the airport here and they don't know the cause of it yet. Apparently they had plenty of time to bring the aircraft in and to put the fire out, but the control tower delayed them, according to Al. Some VIP's plane was there. I don't know how much of this is true. Could be rumours. Once it landed, instead of getting the fire engines quickly and getting the people evacuated, they ordered the plane to taxi all the way to the end of the airfield. It was too late by then. The whole fuselage had gone up. They all perished, including the crew. The following day I drove to the other side of the airport and parked the Land Cruiser on a hillock and had a look at it. The top of the fuselage all the way down to the windows was burned out. They were quite efficient putting out the fire by pumping the water in from the top, but it was too late. All those people's journeys ended at their journey's end.'

'Gives me goose pimples, boy.'

'It frightens me too. Al went inside the following day to get the bodies out. The smell of singed hair and skin was unbearable. Apparently all the bodies were swollen with eyes open and bulging out like ping-pong balls. The central hospital didn't have a mortuary. So they had to hire several food transport lorries with refrigerators to store the bodies. They took pictures of the burnt bodies and put them on a board outside each lorry.'

'Poor bastards. What a sad way to go.'

'Yes, it's a terrible way to go, David.'

Padma brought a tray of coffee, placed it on the table in front of the settee, exchanged greetings with David, enquired how his family was and went out. Nimal and David sat silently and sipped the coffee.

Chapter 2

Nimal's three-year-old daughter Saman Mali came into the sitting room, sucking her thumb and rubbing the tail of her brown monkey glove puppet against her nose, with the flat monkey's body and limbs dangling placidly upside down. She climbed on to the settee next to Nimal and leaned against him. He put his arm around her, looked at David and smiled. David laughed.

'I almost severed the fingers on her left hand, you know. Twice, in fact.'

David shook his head.

'How?'

'It was about a year ago; we were living in the old apartment, in the crowded Al Salaman area. She used to follow me around all the time. Sometimes I didn't know that she was following me. One morning, I was going into the bathroom, and tried to shut the door. I couldn't get it shut, so I slammed it. Then I heard this wincing noise. I threw open the door and saw this two-foot-tall bow-legged little girl in nappy and pink plastic pants, wearing a little short blouse, waddling away down the corridor towards the bedroom, in her bare feet, whimpering. My heart sank. I went running down and picked her up. Padma came and checked her fingers. Superficially the skin was damaged on one finger, but two fingers started swelling very soon. Padma put ice on the fingers and gave her some paracetamol and she just started to suck the thumb of the other hand and was quiet. Padma said the girl's bones were not completely ossified yet, so they would heal soon, and she could still bend her fingers, so there was no need to take her to the hospital. When I went to work, I couldn't concentrate on what I was doing. So I went home, but the girl was fine.'

'Jesus!' David said.

'Second time was when we were in a jumbo jet, flying back to London. I had to take her to the toilet. I took her by the hand, went in, she was following me, and shut the door. "My fingers, my fingers," she was shouting. The concertina door was almost shut but not completely. I panicked. I was trying to feel for the door handle in the dark because the light didn't come on, and it seemed ages before I found it and opened the door, and the same bloody fingers were there. They swelled up and we put ice on them again, and she had a miserable journey. But I was more miserable than she was and could have done with a drink, but the bloody airline wasn't serving any alcohol.'

'Boy, you've been careless.'

'Two narrow escapes.'

'OK, time to go.'

Nimal stroked the little girl's head and told her that he would bring some sweets for her. David picked up the bottle of *sadeki*, and thanked Padma for the coffee. Saman Mali wanted to come with Nimal and David, but her mother was firm. Nimal and David came out of the apartment on to the second floor and walked over to the elevator.

'It's getting very hot. You feel the change as soon as you come out of the air-conditioned apartment,' Nimal said.

'I'm sorry, I must smell like a whorehouse,' David said, raising his arms and sniffing under each armpit. 'Soap ran out, I had to use some of my wife's,' he guffawed, shaking in his tight white Arabic *thorbe*.

'I'm not going to kiss you, boy. By the way, is it true that you have these business cards that you give to women that say "I fire blank shots!" Is it true? I heard that when you went home to New York on holiday, you had a vasectomy done.'

David started laughing as the doors of the elevator opened. Nimal followed him in and pressed the ground-floor button. Mohammed Sofail was already inside, in white *thorbe* and *gutra*. The doors closed and the elevator started going down.

'Salaam alaykum, Mohammed.'

'Wa-alaykum is-salaam.'

'Are you on call today, Mohammed?'

'Yes. Very very busy. All the time they say: "Mohammed, I want this", "Mohammed, I want this." No rest.

No rest. No breakfast yet. Now I am going again. They want some electrolytes and cardiac enzymes done. Ohhh,' Mohammed Sofail said, shaking his head, and throwing his hands in the air.

'Friday mornings are always busy. Usually in the afternoon it quietens down a bit.'

The elevator door opened. Nimal came out, followed by Mohammed and David.

'Hope you have a quiet day, Mohammed.'

'Al Hamdulillah, Shukran.'

Mohammed hurried away towards the main entrance. About the same time, from the second elevator an Egyptian nurse and her escort came out and started to walk towards the entrance. The nurse was in her white trouser uniform. The dark blue stripe on her turban indicated that she was a senior nursing sister.

'What an ass,' David whispered to Nimal.

'That's good living. They eat well. There is not much else to do anyway, locked up there in the nurses' home when they are not working. One of our Egyptian girls in the laboratory was eating stuffed vine leaves the other day. She gave me some. That was the first time I had tasted them. Excellent. Rice mixed with minced lamb mixed with tomatoes, onions, herbs and garlic, olive oil, wrapped in vine leaves and cooked in the oven. You get different tastes on your tongue, from sour to spicy to sweet tastes. The aroma is extremely appetising. They do not add any sauces to their food. They don't have to. Have you tried them, David?'

'What, the food? No, but I will one of these days. I eat anything, boy, except dogs and shit.'

'The next day she brought a whole lunchbox full of stuffed vine leaves to take to my family. They are such generous and kind people. Beautiful girls. Bit stentorian, but lasses unparalleled.'

'If you say so.'

Nimal and David walked towards the side entrance, towards the waste ground where their vehicles were parked.

'He's up early,' Nimal said, pointing to the switchboard man, who sat in his glass-windowed room, shouting down the phone.

They walked down the steps, and stood on the pavement under the orange awning for a moment to allow a local in a white *thorbe* and *gutra* and his wife covered with a black *abaya*, walking on the pavement in tandem, to pass. The morning was torrid. The sun hung above the building at the end of the waste ground on the other side of the road. To their left was the crossroads with humps, and to the right the road went towards the new Movenpick restaurant and bore right again towards the airport road.

They crossed the road and walked on to the waste ground.

'Are we going in yours or mine?' Nimal asked.

'We have to go in yours. The head gasket went on mine. I think the engine head and the valves need replacing as well. The whole shebang is a mess. But I like the old boneshaker Nissan Patrol.'

'Now, be careful where you stand, David. I saw a guy crouching down there, not far from where you're standing.'

'Shit,' David said, quickly looking down and around his feet, and lifting one foot at a time and checking the soles of each shoe in turn. 'It's really funky around here. Anyhow, lucky today,' he said, opening the passenger door, wiping the dust off the black vinyl seat cover with a piece of rag and getting in. Nimal climbed in from the other side and started up the Land Cruiser. He reversed on to the road, then started driving towards the crossroads, where he turned left and started driving towards the airport road.

'I like Fridays,' Nimal said. 'It's a pleasure driving when the roads are not busy. No people around. Only tarred roads, brown walls, brown houses, parched grass and palm trees.'

'This is the best day of the week. Rest day for the workers without wives. The wives of the married ones are waiting to be taken out.'

'They ought to allow women to drive,' Nimal said.

'Never in our lifetime.'

'That skip there is a total health hazard,' Nimal said, pointing to a forty-foot skip parked on the side of the road.

'They throw all the hospital waste in there. Blood-soaked swabs and gauze, used intravenous needles. Dr Ahamed from our lab said he saw an amputated leg in there the other day and the cats were working on it.'

'They don't have any incinerators. So they take the waste to the desert and chuck it there. They don't bury these things. The wind blows the infected material everywhere, contaminating everything, including the water holes.'

'Too much change coming too fast, and they don't have the infrastructure to cope with it.'

'I need to get something to drink. There's a cafeteria just around the corner on the airport road,' Nimal said.

At the give-way he turned the Land Cruiser to the right, drove on about one hundred yards and stopped in front of a small cafeteria.

The dual carriageway airport road was quiet, with only a few vehicles travelling in either direction. Embellished yellow taxis with religious verses written in big Arabic letters on the back windows, and Arabic music playing for the whole metropolis, were overtaking every vehicle in front. The long islands that separated the two carriageways were scantily covered with grass and date palm trees, their pinnate leaves covered with dust.

'I wish I had brought a hat,' David said, getting out of the jeep.

'Yes. It's going to be a very hot day,' Nimal replied.

Two Yemenis were busy inside the café. There were a couple of white plastic buckets on the floor, one filled with chopped-up liver and the other with sliced onions. One Yemeni was cleaning the black metal plate where they fried the liver, and the other was filling the glass-fronted fridge with cans and bottles of soft drinks.

'Sabah il-khayr,' Nimal said, and both Yemenis returned the greeting. David went over to the refrigerator and took out two bottles of Coca Cola, opened them with the bottle opener hanging from a string on the refrigerator door, handed one bottle to Nimal and drank a few gulps from his own.

'Not very cold.'

'He's just putting them in.'

'Every time I drink a bottle of Coke, I remember something funny,' David said.

'What?'

'I'll tell you when we get back to the jeep. Some of these guys understand English.'

Nimal picked two cans from the refrigerator, paid for them, and quickly downed the contents of his own bottle, dropping the empty in the crate on the floor. He followed David back to the Land Cruiser.

'I was working in the accident and emergency department in a hospital in New York a few years ago. One night, well, it was gone midnight, I saw this Puerto Rican geek hovering near the entrance. It looked like he wanted to come in, but was hesitant. I watched him for a while. It seemed he was distressed and he was in pain. I called him in and asked him to sit down. But he wouldn't. He wouldn't speak either. Just kept shaking his head. Anyway, later we found out two black dorks had gotten hold of him and shoved a bottle of Coca Cola up his ass. Oh boy. Oh boy. It was a job getting that out. Poor guy! He was very grateful.' David laughed loudly as Nimal shook his head in disbelief.

Nimal edged the Land Cruiser towards a gap between the islands, did a U-turn on to the other carriageway and headed back towards the market area in the old city centre.

When they arrived, all the shops and offices that lined the road were shut. They passed the vegetable *souk*, and the canvas *souk*. The streets were empty apart from the occasional street urchin, or beggar women in black *abayas*.

'Apparently that belongs to the crown prince,' Nimal said, pointing towards a deserted construction site.

'Most probably when that is finished all these shops will be shifted and these old buildings will be flattened,' David said. 'It's all happening so fast, and the locals cannot keep up.'

'Hey, we are almost there,' Nimal said.

'The whole area is like a medieval town,' David said, looking around.

In the old town, square single- or double-storey flat-roofed mud buildings lined both sides of the narrow streets. Most were shops, now with their metal shutters pulled down. Some of the buildings were derelict, collapsed walls exposing the straw and the reeds and the crudely cut wood used to build them.

The road was clay now, narrowing at times to a single lane with only about a foot spare on either side. Thin streams of waste water ran down the slope. They drove past the old mud sconce with a roughly made wooden door. Rusting spear blades, aimed at some of the previous occupants when sprinting inside while the door was closing, their *thorbes* held high above their haunches, were still embedded in the wood. There was a guard in a khaki uniform standing lethargically outside the door, holding a rifle with one hand. They drove down the street where electrical items and watches were sold, and towards the clock tower in the square. When they arrived, Nimal found somewhere to park and they sat for a moment looking at the crowd of people in front of the mosque.

'There we are. Looks like the crowd is gathering already. The army and the police as well,' Nimal said.

'Let's get down and stretch our legs,' David said, opening the door.

'What about your water bottle?' Nimal said, looking seriously at David.

'It's behind the seat. Don't worry. It'll be all right.'

Nimal got out, shut the door and climbed on to the bonnet of the Land Cruiser, with his legs resting on the front bumper. David climbed up next to him.

'They're just about to start the midday orisons. The prayer call for the faithful,' Nimal said, pointing to the four loudhailers tied to the minaret.

'Look at the clear blue sky, not a speck of a cloud.'

'Do you see the aeroplane up there?'

'Beautiful. It looks like a moving silver spindle with white threads of smoke freezing behind it.'

'I wonder where they're going?'

'North. Definitely north. Another hour or two, probably they will be flying over the Alps.'

'There must be a lot of passengers in it.'

'Must be.'

'How high do you think they are flying?'

'Thirty, maybe thirty-two thousand feet,' David said.

'They must be getting ready to have their lunch.'

'Or breakfast. Or supper. Depends where they are coming from.'

'Yes.'

'Let's say they're getting ready to have their lunch, just like down here, and we're in that plane.'

'OK,' Nimal said.

'The stewardess is pushing the drinks trolley down the aisle now.'

'Are we in first class or economy?'

'Economy, but the drinks are free. When that angel comes to you and asks you, with the gentlest, most beautiful smile in the world: "What would you like to drink, sir?" what would your answer be?'

'Is it one of the local planes? If it is, they don't serve alcohol.'

'Forget it is a damn local plane. It's a plane, a proper plane, serving proper food and proper drink. What's the goddamn drink you would ask from that beauty?' David said annoyingly, raising his voice.

'Whisky,' Nimal said.

'Whisky? It's too damn early in the day. You want to

start with something smooth, like a glass of wine, as a foundation.'

'No. I definitely want a whisky. A large one. A good malt whisky. Neat.'

'Neat. You can't drink whisky neat. It'll burn you. You must put ice or soda or something in it.'

'Not for malt whisky. Don't let the Scots hear what you said just now. They'd be shocked.'

'OK. Have anything you want. I'm going to ask that angel for a chilled glass of white wine.'

'Is that for the woman sitting next to you?' Nimal asked.

'Damn it. I like white wine. I like red wine too. But I prefer white.'

'Well, ask your angel to have one on you as well,' Nimal said, and they both laughed.

'But wait a minute. We forgot one thing. No alcoholic drinks are allowed in this country. It's against the religious law.'

'Yes. The law is for the land. That is the sky.'

'But that air space belongs to this country. It's not right that people are allowed to drink alcohol above this land, inside the country's own territorial air space.'

'That air space keeps changing. A few hours ago it was probably Russia's air space.'

'But right now it's this country's air space and at this moment they are drinking alcohol up there, above the Holy Places. It's what the locals call Haram. Unlawful.'

'Forget that now,' David said. 'What do you think they can see from up there?'

'What they see is what we always see when we fly out from here, or over this country when flying from somewhere else. Undulating brown and red earth, and its shadows when the sun's rays fall on them. Escarpments. Wadis. Circular green farms, patches of palm groves. Scattered small towns, big cities. Rising smoke. Flames from oil wells. That's what they see, if they look down. Not us. Definitely not us. We're too small. Anyway they probably have their blinds drawn down, and are sleeping or watching a film.'

'But we can definitively say the pilot can see below.'

'Yes. Definitely the pilot can see down below. But he's going somewhere. These are only passing glances.'

'Still, we are too small for him to see from that height in the firmament. So he doesn't know that we are here.'

'He knows we are here. He knows there are lots of us down here. But he can't see us. We're too small.'

'But we can see the movement he is making, from down here, and because of that we know that he's up there.'

'That's only if you look up.'

'Of course. Why don't we get a couple of cans of Coke and go and join the crowd and see what those guys are going to do to this scofflaw,' David said.

Chapter 3

The court hearing a week ago had been brief. There were enough witnesses to commit Latifa for adultery. They had caught Hussein Hasmi too.

Latifa was to be put to death by stoning. The sentence was to be carried out the following Friday after the midday prayers.

They sentenced Hussein Hasmi to death by beheading. That was to be carried out the same day.

The soldiers with their Kalashnikovs over their shoulders started to clear the middle area of the car park. They ordered the crowd to move and formed a semicircle to keep them back. Then they cleared a path from the car park to the Palace of Justice, lining up on both sides all the way up to the steps. *Mutawahs* in khaki uniforms, with their long canes waving, were patrolling the path and the cleared area of the car park. Some started mingling with the all-male crowd and some men were elbowing forward, trying to get to the front for a better view.

The midday prayers were finished. The men who

had been praying inside the large mosque next to the car park were coming out, looking for their slippers and shoes among the pile near the entrance. Some of them joined the crowd in the car park. Others walked back to their cars to go home to their families for lunch.

It was after one. The sun was blazing down on the crowd in the square. Some patches of the tarred car park were melting. In the potholes and cracks some resilient parched grass bushes were growing, out-stretched blades squashed by the tyres and embedded in the tar. The big clock at the top of the tower was showing the time, a long time ago, when it had stopped running. The crowd were careful not to expose their wristwatches to the direct sunlight for fear it would melt the electronic circuits inside and stop them. All the watches and clocks in the now shut, air-conditioned row of shops from the clock tower towards the sconce were running smoothly. The crowd was squinting towards the Palace of Justice for any movement. Some were wiping the sweat from their faces with their *gutras* and fanning themselves with whatever they had in their hands. They were quiet and the air was still.

Hussein Hasmi prayed with two prison guards on the mat in the praying corner of the Palace of Justice. After the prayers they stood up and Hussein hugged both guards. They all had tears in their eyes. They shook their heads up and down silently, sighed and hugged each other again. Hussein started to sob and the guards

22

wiped their tears. They had become friends. Hussein took two folded letters out of his breast pocket and gave them to one of the guards. One was for his mother and the other was for his friend Sayeed, whose friendship he had betrayed by his attack on his wife Latifa. The shanty-town dwellers, led by the *mutawah*, had witnessed them in the desert and had believed that it was a pre-planned *affaire d'amour*. The judges found both guilty of the crime of adultery. They were getting Latifa ready for her punishment in another part of the city, inside a women's prison.

Hussein asked for a glass of water. One of the guards poured some water from a plastic bottle into a tumbler and gave it to him. He held the glass in his hand and looked at the crystal-clear water and the tiny bubbles adhered to the surface. He drank slowly, emptied the last drop and gave the glass back to the guard with the words 'Tayyib, ana khalast'. OK, I've finished.

The guard indicated that it was time to go outside. Hussein shook his head, and the guards bound his hands behind him and tied his *gutra* around his head tightly.

Hussein looked around. A few soldiers with machine guns stood near the shut front door. There was one government official, dressed in a clean white *thorbe* and *gutra*, official papers in his hand, waiting to go outside with Hussein. Three air-conditioners were blowing cold air into the entrance hall, but still Hussein was feeling very hot. Sweat was pouring down and his whole body started to shake uncontrollably. He pressed his lips tight.

He did not want any words or sounds to leave his mouth again.

Ummi. Ummi. Please forgive me, ummi.
Abuuwiy. Please forgive me, abuuwiy, abuuwiy.
My little oukhti, little oukhti, please don't cry.

Two soldiers came and stood either side of Hussein. They held his arms and started to walk him towards the entrance. Another soldier opened the door. The bright sunlight falling through almost blinded them.

Sayeed, my good friend, I betrayed you.
Please forgive me, Latifa. I was damnable.
Dear sweet Latifa, was it your will too?
Please forgive me.
Time is short, short, short.

The guards led Hussein out of the entrance, to the top of the stairs.

Beautiful day. Clear sky. I cannot put my hand over
the eyes but I can squint with my eyes. Tears coming.
Blink fast. Time short. So many people. All silent.
All looking at me, me, me.

The guards started leading Hussein down the steps.

Shaking. Can't stop, stop.

24

Brave, I am. No shaking, no shaking. Hasmis are brave.
Still shaking, I can't help it.
Press foot down hard, hard, on step,
Then next foot, hard.
One, two, three, four, five, no more steps.
Flat path, crowd, faces, eyes, so many.
Run? Not possible. Soldiers. Mutawahs. Many.
Better, now better, breathe deep.
Patter, patter, patter, patter.
Slow down, slow down.
Shorter step, longer life. Shorter step, longer life.

The two soldiers on either side tried to pull Hussein along.

Brain, my brain, sparkling, coruscating.
With thousands of my thoughts.
Memories, flashing, flashing, flashing.
Of all my life, long life, short life.
Ummi, ummi, ummi, my ummi.
Village when little, city, shanty town growing up.
School, school, friends, my friends, dear friends.
I miss you all.
Any of you in the crowd?
I look, I look. Cannot see. I look. Please forgive me.
Nabeil, Hameed, Ahmed, Fahad, Sulleiman,
Mohammed, Faisal, Abdullah, Salem, Rashied.
Friends dear, friends dear. My friends.
Desert, playing, driving trucks.

25

Desert tracks, sand dunes.
I am brave. No shaking now.
Lips tight, tight, very tight. No sound.
People many. Soldiers. Eyes, many.
School. Reading, reading, reading, reading.
Religious books. Holy books, off pat.
God, God, God, compassionate, merciful.
Good, bad, good, bad. Good: heaven. Bad: perdition.
Patter. Patter. Patter. Patter.
Bespatter Hasmis, bespatter Latifa.
Books; blackened pictures, words.
Newspapers; blackened pages, torn pages,
Pictures, articles.
Cover your eyes. Sin. Sin. Sin.
But, not for them.
Kings, queens, princes, princesses.
Other books; dog-eared, banned books,
Secret books, friends, bad books. Girls.
Pictures. Stews. Bangkok. Amsterdam.
Videos, haram, haram, haram.
Harem, not haram, harem not haram.
Raiders, victors, women prisoners.
All wives. No haram.
One wife, four wives, mistresses.
One law for one,
Two laws, many laws, no laws.
One palace, two palaces, many palaces.
Finished palaces, unfinished palaces,
Here, there, everywhere.

Their wealth, my wealth,
All from black-gold.
And none for me.
One law for me,
One law for you.

The guards tugged the slowing prisoner along:

All mighty, merciful, compassionate,
You the munificent,
Conveyer of mercy and compassion,
Where are you?
Justice, nemesis.
Sin, sin, sin, sin.
Venial sin, mortal sin.
My sin, venial sin? Mortal sin?
You made me; you made me, lascivious.
Man, woman, children, adults, children.
My fault, your fault. Why? Why? Why?
Perdition, perdition.
You forgive me not. I forgive you not.
You decide. I decide.
Millions and trillions of thoughts.
So fast, I cannot believe, so fast,
For the last time, last few minutes,
Seconds, milliseconds.
Ummi, ummi, I cannot say not to grieve.
I know you will, my ummi.
You will wail, I know, sing a threnody, you will.

I see your faces: grimaces of some.
Feel for me.
I see sad faces: thank you, friends,
Some expressionless.
What are you thinking, my friend?
My whole body has become hyperactive.
Every muscle of my body
Pulsating, pulsating.
Thought flashes in my brain very fast,
Hot and sparkling inside for the last time.
I am afraid, ummi, I am afraid.
I will be brave, abuuwiy, I will be brave.
I am a Hasmi, a brave Hasmi.

The soldiers brought the prisoner to the middle of the square. The crowd, several men deep now, was silent. The soldiers lined up behind Hussein, and the official in white read out the crime he had committed and pronounced the sentence. Suddenly the crowd started clapping. Hussein looked around the faces of the grimacing crowd from left to right, then from right to left. Then he spat at the crowd.

I curse
You all
Ummi
Ummi
Ummi

The soldiers stripped the prisoner to the waist and made him genuflect by pushing him down, then forced his head forward. Hussein could not see the faces now, only feet.

Ummi
Ummi
Afraid
Afraid
Shiver
Shiver
Help
Help
No pain
I see
Your face
Ummi

The executioner came near to Hussein with a long curved sword and stood to his left. Then he raised it and struck as hard as possible. The force of the blow threw Hussein's body forward. The head was not completely severed, but blood started gushing out, bathing his face.

Millions
Of stars
Coruscated
Pain

Hell
Red
Blurred
Suffocating
Hot blood
Ground
Red sky
Ummi
Ummi
Ummi

The executioner raised the sword again and per-formed the *coup de grâce* – execution with compassion.

Air
Ummi
Love
Um—

The desecration of the tabernacle was complete. The executioner wiped the blood from the sword blade on Hussein's clothes and quietly walked away. The official stood there for a little longer and then walked back to the Palace of Justice. The crowd stood in silence, looking at the decapitated body of the prisoner. His head lay with a fixed gaze towards the sky and blood clotting inside his eyes and mouth agape.

After about ten minutes, a police van reversed into the centre of the square, the back door was opened, and two policemen pulled out a stretcher. The prisoner's body was loaded on to it, and a third policeman picked up the head by his *gutra* and placed it alongside the body. They loaded the stretcher into the van, closed the back doors and drove off slowly. The crowd started to clap loudly.

Most of the crowd began to disperse. Some stayed staring at the pool of blood.

The blood had clotted like blobs of jelly, and the serum was flowing among the cracks in the tar, bathing the scanty bushes of grass. The grass roots were busy absorbing the water as fast as they could before it got soaked into the soil or evaporated. The hub of the solar system, the awesome conflagration and the sustainer of life, was far away; while keeping one half of the earth dark, it was illuminating the other half with its energy, and was helping the parched grass bushes in the car park of the square, and other plants and trees everywhere else under its illumination, to combine water with carbon dioxide from the atmosphere to produce food. The omnipotent Hub of the Universe was supposed to be ubiquitous.

Chapter 4

Sayeed opened his eyes. He could see the ceiling fan above, moving fast. Further down to the left, another ceiling fan, but still. He saw a bluebottle fly, hovering above his bed, trying to land on his sheet, then flying up, wings whizzing, zigzagging over the white bed. It landed on the middle of the bed and started to rub and clean its wings with its hind legs. Then it started to clean its eyes with its legs. After a few seconds' pause, it started walking slowly up the bed, towards Sayeed's face. He watched the fly walking on the crisp white bed sheet. It would stop now and then, bring its forelegs together as if it was praying, then rub them together, tilt its head forward, then sideways, focus its compound eyes on Sayeed's head, then proceed forward. Sayeed wanted to flick it away and he tried to move his right hand out of the sheet, but he could not. Then he tried to take the left hand out. He could not move that either. He tried to move his legs. He could not. Then he realised his hands and legs were tied to the bed.

He raised his head and blew at the fly. It flew away. He looked around and saw the rows of beds on either side of him and understood that he was in a hospital ward. He looked down to the nursing station room at the end of the ward to the right. He could see a nurse sitting there. It was bright outside, with sunshine falling on the date palm fronds, just outside the clear glass windows above the row of beds in front of him. He could see a man with a gas mask over his mouth at the end of the front row of beds on the right. In the other beds patients were reading books or newspapers. Most of the patients were sleeping. It must be the afternoon, Sayeed thought. He could not remember how he'd got to the hospital or why his hands and legs were tied to the bed.

Sayeed raised his head and called for the nurse. He could see the nurse stand up, and some patients turned their heads towards his bed. Nura, the Egyptian nurse who also worked in the laboratory, came running towards Sayeed's bed.

'Sayeed, you are awake. Kayf haalak?' she said, chewing gum and with a smile on her face.

'Al-hamdulillaah. Shukran. Untie me, Nura,' Sayeed said.

'I'll have to ask the sister in charge.'

'Why am I tied?'

'You were very ill and restless, fighting with all of us. The dùktoors gave you medicine and you slept almost a week, Sayeed,' Nura said, smiling.

'I'm not going to fight with you, Nura, you know me. Untie me. It hurts.'

'You promise to behave yourself?'

'Yes. Of course, Nura.'

'I'll go and ask the sister. And I'll phone the laboratory to say that you are awake. Your friend Abdul Mubarak asked me to phone him as soon as you woke up. His wife is looking after your little stepdaughter Leila. All your family from the village is here. They are staying with Abdul.'

'What? Why should Abdul Mubarak's wife be looking after Leila? Why is my family here? Where's my wife, Latifa?'

'You cannot remember? May God give you strength – aLLah ya'aafiyk. Your brother and his two wives were here every day to see you. But you were semi-conscious. I am going to phone Abdul. I'll be back soon.'

'Untie me before you go.'

'I'll be back soon,' Nura said, and she ran to the nurses' office and telephoned Abdul Mubarak. He was having his afternoon glass of tea, sitting pensively in the staff sitting room, when she rang. He put on his *gutra* and started running along to the hospital, which was just next door. He ran up to the first floor and went up to Sayeed's bed.

'Sayeed. Kayf haalak?'

'Tayyib. Shukran. Untie me, Abdul.'

'Why don't you untie him now? He's all right,' Abdul said to Nura.

'I'll have to ask Sister Ulfat.'

'Where is she?'

'Gone to lunch. She'll be back soon.'

'We can't wait until she comes. I'm going to do it now,' Abdul said, and he started to untie him.

'Dùktoor Abdul, I'll get into trouble with Sister Ulfat.'

'Don't worry. I'll speak to her.'

Nura slowly walked back towards the nurses' office. Abdul untied Sayeed's hands and legs and he sat up on the bed. They hugged each other. Abdul had tears in his eyes.

'Why am I here, Abdul? They tell me my family is staying with you, and Leila is with your wife. I cannot remember anything. Is everyone all right? Where's Latifa?'

'My poor dear friend, you cannot remember, can you? My dear, dear friend,' Abdul said, and hugged Sayeed again and started to sob. 'You were found in the desert, bedraggled, two days after you went missing. You were barely alive. Unconscious. Perhaps it's good that you don't remember. I am afraid it might come to you soon. Don't worry; the nurses here will take good care of you. They're good nurses. You were very restless and you hit several nurses. One of the Egyptian nurses had her spectacles broken.'

'Me? Hitting nurses? Are you joking?'

'You were very ill and dehydrated and confused and you didn't know what you were doing. You were pulling the intravenous infusion needles out. That's why they tied you up. For your safety and their safety. You're not going to try anything again, are you?'

'Of course not.'

'You'd better not. Otherwise they'll tie you up again, and dose you up too.'

'I promise. Tell me what happened to me.'

'When you are a bit better.'

'I'm all right now.'

'We will wait just a bit longer.'

Chapter 5

Abdul Rahaman came out of the tent. It was still very dark in the desert. The bright lights of the city glowed in the sky to the west. The waning moon above illuminated the black animal hair tent. The camel herd was crouching left of the tent with their heads raised up, shaking and munching their fodder and blowing their nostrils. The sky to the east was a slight glow, and Abdul's Toyota pick-up truck was parked next to his father's GMC Classic Sierra, to the right of the tent. Around that a small herd of sheep and goats was lying.

The night had been cold. Abdul, with a blanket over his shoulders, walked among the bleating goats and sheep. He sat on the back bumper of his truck, lit a cigarette, pulled a long breath of smoke and looked at the pulsating bright stars in the clear sky. The lights that left the stellar assemblage millions of years ago were reaching his eyes now.

He was looking to the past. As the lights were leaving the stars above, down below this land was much different. Ice ages came and went, and during the last ice age the sea level was over one hundred metres below the current level. Climatic changes were turning most of the land into an arid desert. Animals moved freely in all directions, east and west, north and south. Some species survived and others became extinct. The most successful survivor was a latecomer who became the master of the desert; the ancestors of the great august race of Abdul Rahaman, the Bedouins of the desert.

Abdul Rahaman's ancestors were thinkers, philosophers, mathematicians, artists, poets and writers. Their refulgent wisdom radiated from this navel of the earth, in all directions. Travellers were passing in their camel caravans on their way somewhere, or traders who brought goods for barter, and some went back and some stayed. But they also brought different ideas, philosophies and answers to common questions. They were free thinkers sharing free thoughts with free people. Monotheism replaced all that, and if Abdul Rahaman deviated from that now, he would be ostracised as an apostate, charged, sentenced to death, and executed. When the light that left the stars now approached the earth in the future, possibly some of Abdul Rahaman's descendants could still dominate this land, in some form or other. Probably they would be totally free thinkers again, and probably some of them would be passing the oncoming light before it reached the earth, while on their way to somewhere else.

Abdul Rahaman could hear his grandmother and grandfather snoring in the tent behind him. His parents, two sisters and younger brother slept there too. He could see the outline of an aircraft descending like a great big black bird approaching to land on the city. Its flashing lights were rhythmic and the backward thrusts of the engines broke the silence of the desert. He flicked the cigarette towards the goats, walked back to the tent and lay on his foam mattress, covered himself with the blanket and tried to sleep. He couldn't. His mind was restless. He wanted to buy a black Pontiac Trans Am, like his friend Fahad's. But he hadn't enough money. His friend's Trans Am was so powerful; when you pressed the accelerator, the wheels turned so fast, burrowing down into the sand, before it shot off. When you drove it on the flat hard ground, it glided as if it was flying with the engine roaring. Then if you hit a hump, it shot up and flew for a long distance before it landed with a thump, with the heads of people inside touching the top.

Abdul sighed and pulled the blanket over his head. His grandparents and his parents wanted him to get married; now he was almost eighteen. He would have liked to marry Fatima, a girl from their own tribe and a cousin. But that cost money too, for a dowry and other expenses, like jewellery for the bride. The government subsidy for their camels was not very high. Camels were not used for transport any more, only for milk and meat. There was factory farming of animals, and they also imported live animals and meat. Life was getting more and more difficult for the Bedu.

His ancestors used to collect toll from the camel caravans in the old days. There were no travelling camel caravans any more. Everyone travelled in motor vehicles. In the old days, when times were hard, they also used to foray into other tribes, kill all the males and claim all their animals and women, and then the women were their possessions and became their wives and concubines. Those things were not legal any more, so life was very difficult and monotonous, especially now they had to work hard and save hard for a dowry to get a woman. The only adventure available was driving pick-up trucks in the desert like suicide bombers and shooting at every moving or stationary wild animal with rifles.

Several times he had thought of going to the city and working for someone as a labourer. One of his friends who worked in the city said it was good money. But he was a descendant of a very proud Bedu family. They never worked for anyone. They only obeyed their elders and worked as a family unit and as a tribal unit. He could not sell his pick-up truck to buy a Trans Am, because they needed the vehicle to transport camels and other animals to the animal *souks* for selling. There were plenty of used Trans Ams in the car *souks* in the desert, but still they were very expensive. Abdul tried to imagine himself driving his own Trans Am, making a thundering noise on a smooth road, then turning into the desert and driving on the uneven sandy soft ground, with the car getting thrown up and down, steering round bushes and shrubs and driving in *wadis*, avoiding rocks and stones, climbing sand dunes, then accelerating down steep slopes of sand. He sighed again and turned on to his left side.

He could see a faint glimmer of light filtering through the gaps in the tent wall and then heard the sound of his grandfather getting up. Grandfather knew exactly when it was prayer time. He did not need a clock to tell the time. Now he was almost ninety, his health was failing and his eyesight was not very good. Abdul's grandmother was nearly sixty-five. She was from a different tribe and had been abducted when she was a fourteen-year-old girl by his grandfather's tribe after a foray into her village. She was still in good health and very active in doing the domestic work with his mother and caring for the animals.

'Salah, salah. Yallah, yallah,' his grandfather yelled, coming into the middle of the tent. Abdul Rahaman woke his brothers and they all went outside. His parents and grandmother also came out of the tent and they all walked away into the semi-darkness in different directions. When they came back, the men and male children went over to a metal barrel full of water. Using plastic jugs, while one was pouring the water the other started to wash. The women went to the other side of the tent near to another barrel of water for their pre-prayer wash. They brushed their teeth with wood sticks and rinsed their mouths with water. They blew their noses and tried to push water up their nostrils. Cleaned their ears, rubbed some water on their hair and washed their feet.

All the females went inside to pray, but the males prayed outside on a plastic prayer mat. The sun was about to come up over the horizon. They could see the desert all around them beginning to clear. It was peaceful and still.

This was the desert they saw from the time they were born till death, in mild sun in winter, in intense sun in summer, during heavy winds when the tents were brought down, during suffocating sand storms when the air was saturated with fine sand particles, in heavy rain, when the earth around them smelled like water in a new terracotta jug and water dripped through the roof day and night, *wadis* becoming rivers, and afterwards plant and animal life coming alive with flowers of numberless colours sprouting all around, attracting beautiful butterflies and other insects so that the survival of the species could continue. Suddenly ancient species of fish and other fresh water crustaceans would come alive in the pools, as if spontaneous generation was taking place. Observing all this around them, they acquired an encyclopedic knowledge of their world.

Abdul's grandfather sat in his usual place, in the middle of the tent, his back against the central pole, his left elbow resting on a rectangular cushion, twiddling his prayer beads in his right hand, cross-legged on the carpet and looking outside through the main middle entrance of the tent. It could get very hot under the black tent with all sides closed. So in the late morning they would roll up the sides to cool it down. On his grandfather's left sat Abdul Rahaman and his brother, with their father on his right. They all had similar cushions to rest their elbows on.

'It's going to be very hot today. Take the animals to the east side of the Wadi Hassifa,' Grandfather said.

'Not much to graze there either,' Abdul Rahaman's father said.

'If things are bad, we might have to buy some fodder from the city,' Grandfather said.

'It's too expensive. We can't afford it. We might have to take the animals down east of Wadi Hassifa.'

'Perhaps Abdul Rahaman can drive down that way and check whether there is enough greenery.'

'Yes, Grandfather, I will do that today. I know an area with an abundant tamarisk, andaab, hadha, arrad bushes and gahaf trees, down east of Wadi Hassifa,' Abdul Rahaman said.

'I know that too, my grandson, but no one is allowed to graze their animals there. It is a hyma. The hymas are as ancient as our people. They were set aside by our ancestors for the protection of plant and animal life, for our own survival, to use when there are exceptionally bad times, when there is nothing else available,' the old man said.

Abdul Rahaman's grandmother brought in a tray with four small handleless white china teacups filled to the brim with plain tea, put it in front of the grandfather and left. The old man gave a cup to his son, then one to Abdul Rahaman and one to his brother. They all said a prayer, took a sip each of the very hot syrupy tea and put the cups down again on the tray.

'Grandfather, after breakfast I'd like to go and hunt,' Abdul Rahaman said. 'Early in the morning, you see a lot of animals come out to warm themselves after a very cold night. You see lots of chameleons everywhere. I'd like to drive around and see. Perhaps I might find a good grazing area as well.'

'Don't drive too fast. It is too dangerous. You might kill yourself.'

'I cannot drive fast in that pick-up. But I will drive fast when I get my Trans Am.'

'What's that?'

'It's a Sierra. It looks like a giant black beetle. Bigger than my pick-up. And it can almost fly, just above the ground, Grandfather,' Abdul Rahaman said laughingly, and they all laughed.

'This boy is a dreamer. Dream well, boy, about good things. Always follow the Holy Book's guidance. Then you cannot go wrong. Don't get into the wrong crowd and get corrupted. I heard they sentenced a Hasmi to death for adultery. They were always a bad lot, the whole tribe of them. They are the sweepings of the desert. They have bad blood. So be good and at the same time enjoy life, because all these things are given to you to enjoy and be happy. But be abstinent and continent. These are our great virtues.' Abdul

Rahaman looked at his young brother and winked. 'All right, go and hunt. I will be waiting for some fresh meat for my lunch.' His grandfather smiled.

After tea, they had freshly ground and boiled coffee, and freshly baked bread with feta cheese, olives and some leftover goat meat.

Abdul Rahaman was given permission to get up. He went and picked up his Enfield rifle and two boxes of bullets. Then he put his *gutra* on, went to the Toyota pick-up and started to drive to the middle of the desert. The sun was up now. He drove slowly and quietly, watching the ground carefully. It was quiet all around. He stopped the truck, loaded the rifle, and rested the barrel on the driver's-side open window. He held it with the left hand and the steering wheel with his right and started to drive to a flat area where some of the large sand pebbles shone like crystals when the sun fell on them. He had met some white foreigners there several times in the past. This area was about ten kilometres from their tent. The white people had told them that these shiny stones were desert diamonds. They took them away to get them cut, to use in jewellery for their women. Abdul Rahaman laughed at them because Bedus believed that they were only sand pebbles. But he had seen some animals there in the past. When he reached the flat shiny sand pebble area he slowed down, almost to a crawling speed, and watched in front, both sides, and listened. No foreigners there today and the whole area was quiet all around, all the way to the horizon on this hard flat ground. He was careful not to make any dust clouds behind him.

Then, suddenly, he saw some movement on his right. A large gecko was running fast. He turned his pick-up truck and started chasing the animal. It started running in a zigzagged way, trying to avoid the truck. He drove the truck on to the right side of the gecko and started to take aim. It was difficult with the animal meandering and the rifle shaking. Then he raised the rifle, rested it on his left shoulder, took aim again, kept it steady as much as he could and fired. The gecko got thrown over, rolled over several times and came to rest on its back with its yellow underbelly upwards. Abdul Rahaman stopped the pick-up, got out and kicked the gecko over. It was not moving. The bullet had hit its neck. Its eyes were open.

He picked the gecko up and threw it into the back of the pick-up, then laughed loudly, loaded the rifle again and shot the air. He put an audio cassette in his player, turned the volume up and started the engine, singing the same words as the female Egyptian singer. He was taking a different route, and he could see the new highway far away in the desert. It was getting busy with vehicles travelling fast in both directions. He thought of joining the highway and driving south, cutting across the desert to their tent. When he was about five kilometres away from the road he saw a dead animal on the desert track in front of him.

Abdul Rahaman thought of driving fast and running

over it. But when he came nearer he realised that it was not an animal but a dead man. His ragged body was covered with a thin layer of dust. He stopped and got out. He went near the man and, with his foot, slowly moved the man's head. Then he saw a movement in the man; one of his hands moved. He quickly crouched down and started to shake the man by his shoulders. There was no response. He went back to his truck, brought a bottle of water and poured some on to the man's mouth. The water went over the mouth but the man didn't drink it. Then Abdul Rahaman opened the man's mouth and poured in some water. Still the man did not drink. He was breathing slowly. Abdul Rahaman opened the back door of the pick-up, and carried the man over and laid him down next to the gecko. He set off, driving steadily and careful not to bump the vehicle too much.

When he got back he called everyone over. They carried the man inside, laid him on the carpet, and the women started to sponge his body with cool water. They opened his mouth and dropped water slowly from a teaspoon down his throat. But the man was unconscious. Abdul Rahaman's father checked the man's pockets and found his identity card. His name was Sayeed Al Rasheed, he read, and he worked at a hospital in the city. The grandfather ordered his son and Abdul Rahaman to take the man to the same hospital immediately. They put a foam mattress in the back of his father's Sierra and Abdul sat with the man as his father drove. When they reached the hospital, they handed him over to the nurses there. The nurses and the doctor thanked them both and quickly transferred Sayeed on to a trolley, took him to a ward and put a saline drip up.

That was just over a week ago.

Chapter 6

Leila sat cross-legged on the floor, watching the television's only channel, which was showing Japanese cartoons dubbed into Arabic. She was watching the adventures of a little girl, Lena, and a little boy, Adnan, and she was singing the songs the cartoon characters were singing, shaking her head from side to side, swinging her two short plaits with red bows tied to their ends and clapping her little hands. The video recorder below the TV set was recording the programme, so that she could watch it again whenever she wanted. Halfway through, the programme suddenly stopped and the evening prayer call started, showing pictures of the Holy Places.

Leila started to cry. She wanted to know what Lena and Adnan were going to do in their adventure through the forest. Abdul Mubarak's wife, Fatima, came running into the room. She knew what had happened but there was nothing she could do. She took Leila into the kitchen with her where Akila and Halima, Sayeed's sisters-in-law, were cooking. Leila opened the refrigerator door, took a bottle of Vimto out and asked Fatima to open it. She opened the bottle and filled a tall red plastic tumbler. Leila took it and went out to the veranda.

Sayeed's brother Mustafa was sitting on the carpet, looking down to the garden, six footsteps below, and the rhododendron bushes against the tall adobe wall of the villa. The rays of the setting sun were falling on the other side of the unplastered ashen wall. From where he sat, Mustafa could see new buildings going up all around Abdul Mubarak's villa. Some of the new houses had swimming pools.

Abdul Mubarak had bought this piece of land next to his father's property from a relative. He had taken an interest-free loan from the government to buy the land and build this villa, after the hospital refused to give him an apartment in the new German-built staff residential building. His father had been a wholesale grocer. He now owned a block of apartments in the crowded area of the city, rented out to low-paid foreign workers. He lived in the villa next door with his young son, who was a medical student in the city. The eldest of the three children, his daughter, was a teacher in the city, married to another teacher.

Mustafa got up. The loudhailers on the minaret of the mosque nearby were broadcasting the prayer call. He stroked Leila's head, smiled at her and walked down the veranda steps and through the gate. Abdul Mubarak's father, Abdul Aziz, was coming out of his villa. They exchanged greetings and joined the other males who were walking to the mosque.

'I hear Sayeed is getting better,' Abdul Aziz said.

'Yes. I was very worried about him. He was like a father to me, after our parents died. He brought me up.'

'He's a very lucky man. It's a miracle he survived that long in the desert.'

'We're going to see him tonight. Will you come with us?'

'I wish I could come but I am too old to go out in the evening now.'

'Don't worry. We don't know how to thank you all for your kindness. We came and stayed with your son several times so far and he has been very kind to Sayeed and all of us.'

'People sometimes misunderstand my son. His eyesight is not very good. He is also very short-tempered and fights with anyone who disagrees with him. But he is a very religious, kindhearted boy. He helps many people. Unfortunately he has a bad back now and he is suffering.'

'We're so happy that he and his wife are looking after Leila. I don't think Sayeed can take care of her himself,' Mustafa said.

'My son and his wife have no children. The child will have a better future in the city.'

They took their slippers off, rolled up their *thorbe* sleeves and joined the others in the washing area to have their prayer wash.

After the prayers they came out of the mosque

together and started to walk back to their houses.

'My son wants to take me to England for some plastic surgery on my nose,' Abdul Aziz said.

'What happened to your nose?'

'All my life I have been very conscious of my nose. It is so ugly. As you can see, it is in shreds and most of the front is gone.'

'What happened?'

'I had a nose infection when I was a boy and they cauterised it. I can't describe the pain when they heated up the iron rods and burned the nostrils. They were already very painful with the infection, and I can still see those white-hot metal rods, and the smoke from the burning flesh. The smell of my own flesh burning. I still hate that old biddy who did that. Several people had to hold me down. I was determined to show that I was brave, but I passed out,' Abdul Aziz said.

'This is our traditional treatment. I have a scar on my right leg where they cauterised it for a large purulent wound, when I was a boy,' Mustafa said, laughing.

'They give tablets for that kind of thing now. Life is much better now. I'm too old for plastic surgery, and I don't care any more. When I was young, I was worried whether it would frighten women away, but now, does it matter?' said Abdul Aziz, shaking his head.

They were near Abdul Mubarak's house.

'Are you coming in, Abdul Aziz?'

'I better come and see little Leila.'

Mustafa pushed the gate open and they both walked

up on to the veranda and sat on the carpet. Leila came running out and Abdul Aziz took some sweets from the pocket of his *thorbe* and gave some to her. She laughed and climbed on to his lap.

Chapter 7

When Abdul Mubarak came home it was almost dark. The streetlight just outside the high garden wall lit up the steps and the veranda where Abdul Aziz was still sitting with Leila on his lap. She was tugging his red-hennaed beard with one hand and sucking the thumb of the other. Mustafa sat next to him, smoking a cigarette.

'Salaam alaykum,' Abdul Mubarak said, stamping his feet to shake the sand off.

'Wa-alaykum is-salaam,' they replied. Mustafa got up and hugged Abdul Mubarak.

'He is awake!' Abdul Mubarak cried, throwing up his hands. The women came running to the veranda.

'Did he say anything?' Mustafa asked.

'He wanted me to untie him and I did. He is not struggling or fighting any more. In fact he is back to how he was before. Same old Sayeed.'

'But what did he say?'

'He cannot remember anything.'

'What? What do you mean, he cannot remember?' asked Fatima.

'He is asking for Latifa and Leila. He doesn't seem to know what has happened to him.'

'He will have to shake out of it and face up to what has happened,' Halima said.

Akila started to cry.

'The doctors say that we have to be very careful. They told me not to discuss Latifa with him or anything that happened. They don't know what the shock might do,' Abdul Mubarak said. 'They also said that he will start to remember by himself, and that we have to be prepared to cope with that.'

'We're going to take him home, as soon as he is ready,' Mustafa said.

'He's still very weak. I think it will take at least another week,' Abdul Mubarak said.

'Latifa's family is coming tomorrow to take her body home. I think we must all go with them to the village for her funeral,' Halima said, and all the women started to cry.

'We must not let Sayeed know anything of this yet,' Abdul Mubarak said. 'And I think it would be better not to take the child to the hospital to see Sayeed.'

'Let's eat our supper quickly and then go to the hospital. We don't know what time we'll be back,' Fatima said, walking towards the kitchen with the other women.

Abdul Mubarak took his *gutra* off, wiped his bulging eyes with it, put it over his left shoulder and sat down slowly, trying not to disturb his bad back. He took a

55

bag of sweets from his pocket and gave it to Leila. She took it with a smile, showing her brown decaying stumps of teeth, and started to unwrap a sweet.

'Don't eat that before you have your supper,' Abdul Aziz said.

Leila laughed, put the sweet in her mouth and started munching it with a bulged left cheek.

'This child doesn't listen to anyone. I don't know what she is going to be,' Abdul Aziz said.

Leila pulled his beard hard and laughed. Abdul Mubarak leaned forward and stroked her hair.

The women brought out a large metal plate heaped with rice and chicken, a bowl of water for washing the hands, a jug of drinking water and some glasses, and set it all on the carpet in front of the men. They placed their right hands to their hearts and withdrew back inside. Abdul Aziz sat Leila next to him and told her to wash her right hand. She put both her hands in the bowl and started to splash the water, laughing. Abdul Aziz told her to stop, washed his own hand and passed the bowl to the other two. They ate slowly and silently from the same plate. Leila ate a few mouthfuls of rice, but refused to eat any chicken. The women ate inside.

After the meal, everyone got ready to go to the hospital. The women wore their long black dresses and covered themselves with *abayas*. Abdul Aziz said he would stay at home with Leila until they came back. The child was falling asleep by this time and did not make a fuss. The women followed the men out, holding their long skirts up over their ankles, down the steps and out of the gate. They climbed into the back of Abdul Mubarak's Chevrolet Caprice Classic, which was parked outside the gate. Mustafa sat in the front with Abdul, and he said a prayer, touched the steering wheel with both hands, and started the car. He drove towards the dual carriageway. Cars were parked on both sides of the side road, making it narrow. From a fluorescent-lit cafeteria on the left, music blared out from the speakers facing the road.

An oncoming Range Rover driven by a young local man blocked Abdul's path. There was enough room only for a single vehicle to pass. The young man in the Range Rover pressed his horn several times, signalling Abdul to reverse, and then he came and stopped almost touching the front of Abdul's car. Abdul stopped the engine, got out and shouted at the young man to reverse. The young man got out and sat on the bonnet of his car, folded his arms and smiled. Abdul was screaming that they were late visiting a sick man, but the young driver looked unconcerned. A queue of vehicles was building up behind. With sweat pouring down, Abdul came back in and turned the engine on to get the air-conditioner running. People were coming out of the café to watch the fracas. Finally the queue behind the Range Rover began to reverse.

'You get into your car very peacefully and calmly, but you get out of it transformed into a mad man,' Abdul said.

Mustafa laughed and lit a cigarette. The women were giggling. The young driver of the Range Rover was ordered by the other drivers to get back in his vehicle, but he did so reluctantly, lifting his middle finger to Abdul, who put his hand out of the window and returned the gesture vigorously.

Out on the dual carriageway at last, they began to travel easily. Abdul got into the fast lane, pressed the cruise button and took his foot off the accelerator. The reflections on the bonnet were moving fast and the streetlights in the middle islands were coming to him rapidly and disappearing behind him. He looked at Mustafa and smiled.

'This is what I call perfect driving. Not many cars on the road and none in front of you. The lane all to yourself.'

'Aren't you going a bit fast?' Mustafa asked.

'In this car you don't feel the speed,' Abdul said, coming off the cruise control and slowing down slightly. 'I used to have a Mazda hatchback. That was all right. But this is better, especially for long distances. Fatima likes it as well,' he said, stroking the steering wheel.

At the main roundabout he took the turning for the airport, made a U-turn between two islands and drove down to the hospital entrance. At the barrier the guard recognised him and saluted. Abdul drove into the car park, wincing with back pain as the car hit the speed bumps, and parked in a space close to the laboratory.

Mustafa got out and lit a cigarette while he waited

for the others. They started to walk towards the hospital, Halima carrying a stack of food containers and Akila a bottle of grape juice. They went upstairs to the ward where Sayeed was. From near the nurses' station they could see Sayeed lying in bed, hands tucked behind his head. Halima and Akila walked over to him.

'Thank God you are all right, brother,' Akila said, throwing back her veil. Halima threw back hers and looked at Sayeed with tears in her eyes.

'All of you here? Who's looking after the animals and the children?' Sayeed asked, sitting up.

'Never mind that. How are you?' Halima asked gruffly.

'All right. They say that they found me in the desert. But I don't know what I was doing there. I don't remember anything.'

'There's nothing to remember. You were ill and now you're all right. We're going to take you home,' Halima said.

'Dùktoor Fahad has to discharge him first,' Abdul Mubarak said.

Sayeed looked at Mustafa, who stood at the bottom of the bed stroking his beard.

'Kayf haalak?' Sayeed asked.

'Tayyib.'

'Inta?'

'Tayyib.'

'We brought some food,' Halima said, putting the containers on the bed.

59

'I can smell it. Just like home. I'm very hungry. Where are Latifa and Leila?'

'Latifa went to her parents'. She got fed up with the shanty town,' Halima said quickly. 'Would you like to eat now?'

'Where's little Leila?'

'She's with Abdul Mubarak's father. She's fine. Do you want to eat now?'

'I don't understand,' Sayeed said, bending his head and pressing a forefinger and thumb against his eyes. 'I don't remember anything.'

'Sayeed, why don't you eat? You've lost weight. Before they send you home you have to be able to walk. I don't think you can walk now.'

'Yes. I can walk. They took me to the bathroom earlier on. Only ate about an hour ago. Tasteless hospital food. Foreigners' cooking,' Sayeed said, with a smile.

'We're very glad you are getting better. You had us worried.'

'We have to go home tomorrow,' Halima said.

'When are you coming back?' Sayeed asked.

'They don't have to come back. I can take you to the village when you're better,' Abdul Mubarak said.

'Your friend is a very kind man,' Halima said.

Chapter 8

Latifa's parents cried for more than a week after the death sentence was passed. Then the sentence was carried out and it was all over.

Latifa's mother, Salwa, was lying on the carpet by the window in the sitting room. She was holding one of Latifa's dresses, wiping her continuously flowing tears and looking outside. She could see date palm fronds moving slowly in the wind and the clear blue sky above. There was a full glass of milk near her on the floor on a saucer. Latifa's two childhood friends, Fatma and Muna, were sitting on the floor beside her, fanning her with dry palm leaves. There were more women in the kitchen preparing drinks for visitors. Everyone was silent.

Outside on the veranda several men were sitting on the carpet: family friends and neighbours. Some were smoking cigarettes. Each one had a glass of plain tea in front of him, and a plate of dates lay on the carpet. At the border of the white sand yard in front, red and pink Chinese rose bushes, which Latifa had planted next to the picket fence by the road, were now in full bloom.

The date palm grove with its dark green leaves around the bungalow was bathed in the before-noon intense sunlight.

Early in the morning Latifa's father, Al Fawzi, and a friend had taken a van and gone to the city to bring Latifa's body home.

Latifa's father went to the women's prison. A female prison guard took them to an inner room to identify the body. Latifa was laid on the floor swathed in white sheets. They could see only her face, and the patches of seeped-out blood, now dried, stained the sheets below her face. Al Fawzi looked nervously around the room, with a white handkerchief covering his mouth. The female guard pointed her finger at the body on the floor. He sat down and placed his withered hand on Latifa's forehead and touched her swollen closed eyes and stroked the blue face and started to sob uncontrollably. The guard, with a handkerchief covering her nose, asked whether it was his daughter, and when he nodded his head she ordered him to hurry up because it would be prayer time soon. Al Fawzi stood up slowly and looked at the guard. She produced a book and showed him where to sign. Then she brought a black body bag and told the two men to transfer Latifa into the bag. Al Fawzi was still sobbing as the bag was zipped up. She told them to buy some blocks of ice from a nearby shop and to put them inside the bag before they left the city because of the long journey they had to make in the heat. The body had already started to smell very bad. She told them to go quickly before the shop closed for the prayers.

They carried the body to the back of the van, laid it on the floor, placed plastic-wrapped blocks of ice inside the body bag and left for the village. They wanted to be home to bury Latifa before sunset.

In the afternoon Mustafa and his wives arrived home. Halima and Akila got out and looked for their children. Halima's friend, who had been looking after them, was busy in the kitchen. She said that the children were playing in their neighbour's garden with a newborn colt. They thanked her and got back in the truck again. Mustafa started to drive in the *wadi*, heading towards Latifa's bungalow.

When they arrived, a large crowd was gathering. Some were walking in the garden, others were sitting in the veranda or inside the bungalow. Halima and Akila rushed inside while Mustafa walked on to the veranda, where some elderly men were sitting on the carpet. He exchanged greetings with everyone and sat on the floor.

Inside, Salwa was sitting cross-legged, her hands clenched tight on her lap, looking at everyone's faces and swaying her body forwards and backwards. Fatma and Muna were sitting on either side of her, cross-legged and facing each other. Halima and Akila threw back their veils. When Salwa saw them she raised her

63

hands towards them. They both knelt down and hugged and kissed her and she held on to them tight and they all started wailing. Fatma and Muna moved away and Halima and Akila sat on either side of Salwa and they all cried. All the women burst out crying at the same time.

'Oh Haliemaaa, my girl is dead. Oh Akielaaa, my little girl is dead. They killed my beautiful princess. I curse them. Let thunderbolts strike them all,' Salwa wailed in a coarse voice.

'Why kill the innocents? Oh innocent Latifa, you are not guilty. I curse that evil devil Hussein, who ruined her. Let him rot in Hell. This is not justice,' Halima wailed.

Akila was sobbing and wiping her tears with a hand-kerchief. The room was very hot. Halima and Akila took off their *abayas* and threw them on the carpet. Salwa went quiet again and clenched her hands and started to rock her body. She had refused to eat, but sipped some milk now and then. Halima and Akila got up and went towards the kitchen as Fatma and Muna came and sat on either side of Salwa again.

It was just before sunset when Al Fawzi brought his daughter home. While the van was slowly coming up the sand track, all the visitors on the veranda got up and came out to the garden. The women put their veils and *abayas* on and came outside wailing. Salwa got up, supported by Fatma and Muna, and came on to the veranda, wailing, with Halima and Akila behind her. Salwa watched the van turning into the front yard, with Al Fawzi sitting at the front and his friend driving. She started breast-beating and crying loudly, throwing her hands in the air.

They turned the van around and reversed it towards the veranda, then stopped and opened the back doors. A stretcher lay ready on the veranda. They carried it out to the van and put it inside, next to Latifa's body. Two of the mourners climbed into the van, unzipped the body bag and took out the plastic bags full of melted ice. The body bag was zipped up again and placed on the stretcher. The water dripped from it as they carried it to the veranda. The smell was overpowering and some of the onlookers covered their noses. Others went to the lemon bush near by, pulled a few leaves, crushed them and held them to their noses. Al Fawzi came and stood next to Salwa and looked into her face.

'Did you bring our daughter home, husband? How is our baby? Let me see her face,' Salwa wailed. Al Fawzi shook his head and started sobbing.

The sun was going down and the elders told everyone to hurry up because they had to take Latifa to the other side of the big rock for her burial before the sun went down. But Salwa wanted to see Latifa's face. She bent down as Al Fawzi opened the bag. Then she was screaming and kissing Latifa's face as the women pulled her away. They all recited religious verses and prayers. They closed the bag again and went to lift the stretcher to take Latifa away. The women started wailing and Al

Fawzi started crying loudly as they lifted the body out to the front garden. The men followed it and the women stayed behind.

'Are you leaving home for the last time, my sweet daughter?' Salwa wailed, as she watched them carrying her daughter away to the desert to bury her. One of the stretcher poles at the front rested on Al Fawzi's shoulder. He had insisted on carrying his daughter on his shoulders on her last journey. Salwa and all the women watched the pallbearers carrying Latifa away down the path towards the *wadi* and towards the desert. Salwa started beating her breast again and shaking her head, with tiny bubbles of sputum at the corners of her mouth. When they could no longer see the funeral procession, the crowd started to disperse and the women brought Salwa inside and helped her to sit down. Fatma and Muna, wiping their tears, started to fan her.

'I remember you girls when you were little you used to run around in the garden with my sweet girl,' Salwa said, stroking their faces. 'You used to climb trees and sometimes beat up the boys. Do you remember?' Fatma and Muna shook their heads. 'One day Latifa fell out of a tree and she was unconscious. Muna, you came running to me saying Latifa was dead. You must have been about five years old. Latifa had a broken arm. We carried her to the village medicine woman and she had regained consciousness by then. The woman wanted to cauterise her hand to cure her, but I said no. I wasn't going to let her scar my beautiful girl's hand. Al Fawzi

66

put a wood splint on her arm and collected wild leaves, crushed them, heated them up, covered her forearm and bandaged it. Her hand was as good as new after a few weeks. I am glad I did not let that woman scar my little girl. She has beautiful hands.' Salwa smiled, shaking her head up and down, and sighed.

It was dark when the men came back. They sat out on the veranda and the women served them their meal on a large metal plate. They ate silently, sitting under the fluorescent light. The front garden was in complete darkness now. Insects were flying around the two hanging lights on the veranda.

Salwa sat cross-legged, her hands clasped tight on her lap and with tears flowing down. She started swaying forwards and backwards and began to lament:

'Oh my princess talk to me
Oh my princess sing for me
Pick the flowers and dance on sand
Oh my princess look at me.'

Chapter 9

A dejected-looking Nimal sat in the laboratory sitting room, his cheek resting on a folded hand with his elbow resting on the chrome arm of the easy chair. It had been a trying few days. Sayeed's problems had affected everyone. Tempers ran high in the close community of the laboratory. Arguments arose over simple trivialities. Some of the foreign workers wanted to leave but they could not, not until they finished their contracts. The hospital administration office held their passports and they needed exit visas to leave the country.

James MacMurray and George Fielding, two of the Scottish technicians and friends of Nimal, and a colleague came and sat beside him.

'Things are getting a bit serious, son,' Jim said. 'That Iraqi guy has made a complaint against you. The director's office sent me a message to go up there. I think they want a statement from me as well.'

'Bastard.'

'I don't know why he makes such a fuss. I think he wants to get you. This is why he didn't fight back when you fisticuffed him. This is why he went to the Central

Hospital, got some stitches to his face, took a letter from the hospital and went to the police.'

'Bastard.'

'Apparently he's engaged to the hospital director's sister-in-law.'

'Is he really?'

'This is what I heard. Apparently that's why he gets dressed up like a local.'

'Why couldn't he fight like a man and leave it at that? Friday was a very bad day for me. Yankee David and I went to the "chop square" and that was terrible. We still can't get over it. You see, I want to be a writer one day and I wanted to see how I felt watching something horrific like that. I don't think I could go through that again. Mind you, there are regulars who go there to watch the spectacle.'

'Spectacle? I wouldn't want to see something like that for all the oil money in the Middle East. It was a bit weird going there, if I may say so.'

'Abdul Mubarak told me today; the guy who was executed was the one who attacked Sayeed's wife.'

'Fuck's sake.'

'On the way back, David and I drank half a bottle of sadeki and when I got home I ate some lunch and went to sleep. Then Padma woke me up to go to this meal at Ahamed's house.'

'What actually happened?' George said. 'I only heard bits and pieces.'

'We were invited for this meal at Ahamed's and they

invited Jim as well. When we got there Jim wasn't there. So I went to his apartment, which he shares with the Iraqi guy. He said Jim wasn't well and wouldn't let me in. I just ignored him and tried to go in anyway and he tried to push me out. Then I suppose I had a kind of reflex action; my hand hit him and his face scraped along the sharp artexed wall. Just some minor cuts, not a big deal. But the bastard didn't retaliate. He just did the most effeminate thing possible and went to the hospital to show his little scratches to a doctor and then went to the police.'

'He had some cuts inside his mouth as well, he told me. He did have to have some stitches,' James said.

George laughed, and shook his head.

'He ruined our meal that day. Jim only had a hangover. Ahamed's wife's flaming hot curry cured it anyway,' Nimal said.

'That Iraqi guy is weird. I go jogging with him sometimes and he wears this blue jogging gear with "Al Karj" written in big letters on the back in a curve and down the sides of his legs. Before we go jogging on the road, he stands with his legs astride and his hands stretched above on the wall of the staff residential building, like a police suspect's body check position, then he presses to the left hard, then to the right, as if he could topple over the seven-storey edifice with all his Iraqi might. After that he runs as fast as he can on the same spot like a mouse on a treadmill. Then he loosens himself by raising his hands above him and shaking his body. After that he is ready to jog. I sit on the steps and smoke a cigarette while he goes through this ritual every time,' James said, shaking his head.

'Bastard studied in America. He's got a slight American accent too. Probably where he learned not to retaliate, and sue the other guy if possible to get some money,' Nimal said.

'Bloody nancy,' George said.

Mohammed Hasan, the Sudanese technician, came into the sitting room, exchanged greetings with everyone. He made a glass of plain tea for himself, and went and sat quietly in the corner. He took a religious book from a bag and started reading. Nimal and the two Scots went quiet. A few moments later Dr Fatima came in and told Mohammed that there was an urgent blood sample for a full blood count. Mohammed slowly closed his book, kissed it, put it inside the plastic bag, placed it on the table and went to the haematology department.

'Great guy, Mohammed Hasan, such a gentle person,' James said.

'And pitch black. When I bought my first video camera, I was trying it out, and Mohammed came to our apartment that night so I filmed him. With a two-thousand-watt lamp aimed at his face, there still wasn't enough light to film him. His eyes and white teeth came out all right,' Nimal said.

'Most of the Sudanese people are great people,' George said.

'Look at that saintly Mohammed Hasan working away in haematology.'

'He's like a saint now he's in his fifties and still not married. You don't know the half of it though,' George said. 'He worked in a hospital laboratory in Glasgow when he was a young man. The Sudanese government sent him there on a scholarship to get his qualifications. Those days he used to go pubbing with the boys and he had a few girlfriends too. One day the boys took him to see a football match. England against Scotland at Hampden. A great national event. Apparently Mohammed had a Scottish flag wrapped round his neck and he was wearing a top hat with a flag tied around it. The boys saturated him with Tartan beer and he was singing and dancing with two empty cans of beer in his hands.

'Then he committed the ultimate vile crime possible while one has the Scottish flag on oneself. He started cheering the English side. Scots couldn't believe it. They rubbed their eyes and looked at Mohammed to see whether they were dreaming. Of course they were not. So they put him on neat Scotch, straight from the bottle down his throat, and he went mad. He wanted to get on the field, to join the England team, and he wanted to strip. Then he started yowling like a wolf and passed out. After the match, the boys carried their Nilotic son like a dead body on their shoulders with a wreath of empty beer cans on him, singing "Rule Britannia" with substituted words. Mohammed is a completely changed man since then. He has become a teetotaller, and a deeply religious man. I think his brain got damaged slightly.'

Mohammed Hasan finished his blood test, wrote the report and gave it to Dr Fatima and came back into the sitting room. He looked at Nimal and his friends, bent his head slightly and, touching his heart with his right hand, went to the corner slowly and sat down. He took his religious book out of the plastic bag again and started reading it from right to left and back to front.

Chapter 10

It was a long day for Nimal. After he finished his work he came to the sitting room and sat next to Mohammed Hasan, who was on call that day.

'I went to see Sayeed,' Mohammed said.

'How is he? I must go and see him on my way home today.'

'He seems to be all right. He's eating well, and he wants to come to work. He doesn't remember anything, and I just listened to him and said that he should go home to the village as his family had suggested and recuperate before he comes back to work. He said to me that his wife had gone back to her family and the child is with Abdul Mubarak.'

The Egyptian receptionist Magidi brought the 'Iraqi guy', Fakhri, into the staff sitting room. He was looking for Nimal. He came and stood near the door and delivered the police summons discourse.

'I want everyone in this room to witness what I am going to say: I, Fakhri Al Makawi, have been asked by the head of police at Sara Sitteen to deliver this verbal summons to Nimal Jayawardena. You, Nimal Jayawardena, are ordered to report to Sara Sitteen police station today before six thirty p.m. Failing to do so will result in the police coming to arrest you. End of the summons message,' Fakhri said, and went out.

'What the fuck was that?' Nimal asked Jim, who was sitting on the other side.

'I don't know, son. You'd better ask Mohammed.'

'He just delivered the summons for you to attend the police station,' Mohammed said.

'Is it legal? Verbally? Shouldn't it be in writing?' Nimal asked, looking worried.

'It can be in writing, or it can be verbal too. That's the law here. I suppose some people can't read. It's quite legal,' Mohammed said.

'I'm not going anywhere. That idiot is crazy,' Nimal said, sliding down the chair and looking more worried.

Some of Nimal's colleagues, who had heard the commotion, gathered around and started to ask what was happening. They all advised Nimal to go to the police station with an Arabic-speaking person, and warned him that if he did not go, the police definitely would come looking for him. They told him to tell his family before he went and to go prepared, just in case they locked him up. Nimal started sweating. He remembered a story he had heard about an Egyptian man going to see his wife in the hospital who drove his car through red traffic lights and the police threw him in jail. His two little children had been left in his flat on their own. The man had pleaded with the police to let him go. A week later he was released. When he got home, he found both the children dead of thirst, and his wife had died in the hospital too. The man lost his sanity.

'Can you please come with me to the police station, Mohammed?' Nimal asked. Mohammed was a bit hesitant at first because he too was a foreign worker. But in the end he agreed.

Nimal arranged to meet Mohammed on the ground floor, outside his apartment, and went home to explain to his wife. Padma started crying when he told her what had happened. He told her to contact Professor Mohammed Al Farid, the Head of Surgery and a local, also a friend, and ask him to help them. Then he went downstairs. Mohammed Hasan was waiting for him, pacing up and down with his head bowed. They went outside, got into Nimal's Land Cruiser and started driving.

'I'm fed up with this dump, Mohammed,' Nimal said, driving carefully over the humps at the crossroads.

'Yes.'

'I am so fed up. I heard that you're not going to renew your contract.'

'Yes. My parents are getting old. I can get my old job back in the Ministry of Health in Khartoum. Five years here is long enough.'

'I don't know what this Iraqi guy is up to.'

'Yes.'

'Have you thought of getting married?'

'Yes. My parents want me to.'

'Watch this now, Mohammed,' Nimal said, stopping at red traffic lights. A row of vehicles stopped abreast of him. Nimal pressed the accelerator, with the clutch pedal down, and revved the engine hard. Then he started inching forward. All the other vehicles started doing the same – American cars, pick-up trucks, four-wheel drives – inching forward like the cars on a racing track waiting for the green signal. Then, suddenly, one of the pick-up trucks shot forward, through the red traffic lights, zigzagging to avoid colliding with vehicles going across. Nimal started laughing. Mohammed shook his head in disbelief. Finally, when the lights changed, the rest of the vehicles shot forward and started racing to overtake the others. But Nimal drove off at normal speed.

'That was dangerous,' Mohammed said.

'I learned it from the locals.'

'If there is a crash people can get killed. You could get into trouble.'

'They were all doing it.'

'But you started it.'

'Who is going to prove it, Mohammed? It's just a bit of fun.'

'Please don't do it again.'

'OK, Mohammed.'

Nimal parked near the police station at Sara Sitteen and they went inside. At the reception desk Mohammed told the policeman about the verbal summons Nimal had received. The policeman looked in the register and asked them to sit down. Nimal waited nervously and lit up a cigarette. He had stopped smoking a few months before but the worry had made him start again. The policeman at the reception pressed his cigarette butt on to an ashtray overflowing with cigarette ends and lit another cigarette. Most of the people waiting were foreigners. After about an hour the chief police officer came and went through the list of people waiting. Nimal was given a date to attend a court hearing. When he heard this, Nimal became overwrought.

'I don't know what to do now,' he said as he and Mohammed left the police station.

'We have to talk to someone. There's only four days until the court hearing.'

'I might have to get a lawyer. How do you get a lawyer here?'

'You must ask someone.'

Back at the hospital, Nimal thanked Mohammed for his help and went upstairs to his apartment.

'I spoke to Mohammed Al Farid,' Nimal's wife Padmawathi said, as he came in, putting a box of chocolates on the coffee table.

'Yes,' Nimal said, and sat on the settee.

'He was shocked that you could behave like a street fighter. Professional people should behave with dignity, he said.'

'Yes.'

'I am getting fed up. I want to leave here with the children as soon as possible.'

'Yes.'

'This is not the first time, is it? That time when we were coming home from shopping, and it was nearly eleven o'clock at night, when that big American car full of Lebanese, and a local driving it, hit ours and drove away, and you started chasing it in your little car.'

'That's my problem. I dislike injustice. I couldn't let the bastards get away.'

'You chased them. They went through red traffic lights and you went through red traffic lights as well. We were terrified sitting at the back. The children were screaming and I was shouting and you didn't stop.'

'It was a bit silly. It's just the instinctive reaction to injustice.'

'And when their car got stuck in a narrow bend you got out and started to scream at them.'

'Yes, I am really ashamed of that. I used all the filthy words I knew. And he didn't understand English. But some of his Lebanese friends did.'

'There were six Arabs in that car and they were all very big.'

'What matters is not how big you are, but how big you think you are,' Nimal said, laughing.

'I don't know how you can laugh at it. It's not normal at all. Then you didn't let him drive his car and told him that he must go in our car.'

'I didn't want him to escape again. Now I feel ashamed of myself the way I shouted at him and called him bad things to his face.'

'They could have murdered us and no one would ever have been found.'

'It was very foolish, I know, very foolish.'

'Then you took him to the local police station and he agreed to repair our car. That local driver is a decent person. That's why you were lucky,' Padma said.

'Yes, he was a decent guy. You remember he drove us back home in his car after we left ours in his garage for repairs that night.'

'Yes, he was decent. After he brought us home he put his hand on his heart and said something in Arabic. I am sure he said that he was very sorry for all that. Later I discovered that they do these kinds of things for fun. Smashing into other people's cars and driving off. A kind of joy-riding, I suppose.'

'Is Mohammed Al Farid going to help us?' Nimal asked impatiently.

'I haven't finished. A few weeks after the car incident, you slapped Dr Saleem's face.'

'Can we talk about this another time? What did Al Farid say?'

'No. I want to talk about it now. You slapped your head of department's face. That was bad.'

'We had a fight. He is a bastard. Everyone knows that. He hit me. I hit him. His fan belt on top of his gutra went flying. I still feel his scanty whiskers on the back of my hand. I think the snake needs some male hormones. The next day we shook hands and apologised to each other and that was that. It was four years ago. What did the blasted Al Farid say?'

'I feel drained. I cannot take this any more. He is going to speak to the Iraqi gentleman, and he said if necessary he will go to court with you and intercede.'

'Thank God for that.'

'Don't think it's over yet. You could still get thrown in jail.'

'I'm tired. I'm hungry. Is there anything to eat?'

'I will get it ready,' Padma said, and went to the kitchen.

Nimal went to the bedroom. He opened his wife's wardrobe and took a quart bottle of homemade beer out from behind her dresses, brought it to the dining table, filled a large glass to the brim, sat down and started quaffing.

Chapter 11

'Mohammed, can you ask Sayeed whether he needs anything?'

When Mohammed Hasan spoke, Sayeed shook his head and smiled.

'Please tell him that he's looking well.'

'He says, so do you.' Mohammed translated Sayeed's reply.

'Please tell him to go back to his village and have a very good rest.'

'He says Abdul Mubarak is going to take him home tomorrow,' Mohammed replied.

'Our lunch hour is almost finished. We'd better go back, Mohammed,' Nimal said, standing up.

They shook hands with Sayeed, wished him a safe journey home and started walking down the ward towards the nurses' station.

'He's made a remarkable recovery, hasn't he, Mohammed?'

'God looked after him. He's a good man, poor Sayeed.'

'I wish God had looked after his wife too, Mohammed.'

'That was God's will.'

They started walking down the steps.

'Perhaps it's a good thing that he remembers nothing.'

'Perhaps.'

'Probably shock.'

'Yes.'

'I am glad my problems are over,' Nimal said.

'It was a good lesson.'

'I'm so grateful to Dr Al Farid for persuading the Iraqi guy to withdraw the complaint from the police.'

'He has withdrawn his complaint from the hospital too, I heard,' Mohammed said.

'Yes, thank God. What a relief. I am going to see the Iraqi guy and thank him.'

'Is that wise?'

'Yes. Now the matter's closed, I must thank him,' Nimal said, walking into the laboratory with Mohammed.

'You're late back,' Abdul Mubarak growled, looking at his watch. 'I was waiting to go for my lunch.'

'We went to see Sayeed. I hear you're taking him to his village tomorrow.'

'Yes. I'm a bit worried about him, though. They don't have a doctor in the village. Today he said to me that he gets bad dreams in the night and he can't remember them when he wakes up.'

'You have to expect that.'

'He's asking to see Leila. He does not understand why Latifa left her with us. At the same time he's glad that she's in a good house rather than a hovel in the desert. I told him that she is going to school and has lots of friends now, and the poor chap had tears in his eyes.'

'That's good. I better go and do some work.' Nimal got up to go and Abdul Mubarak stopped him.

'I heard the news. I'm glad you aren't going to jail. We're short of staff anyway,' he said, laughing.

That same day, after work, Nimal went and rang the doorbell to Fakhri Al Makawi's apartment. He apologised to him for the trouble and shook hands with him. Nimal said that he was so grateful to him for withdrawing his complaints from the police and also from the hospital. Fakhri smiled.

'Are you free this evening, Fakhri?' Nimal asked.

'Not much to do around here,' Fakhri said in his American accent.

'I would like to take you out for a meal. Would you like to come?'

Fakhri was silent.

'I would like to thank you and I would like to make it up with you. You have been a good gentleman.'

Fakhri puckered his forehead.

'I was thinking of the newly opened Movenpick restaurant, just down the road,' Nimal said.

'I will think about it,' Fakhri said, squinting and twitching his right eye and wrinkling his forehead a bit more.

'I am going upstairs now. I will get ready and come. In the meantime you get ready and we will have a wonderful meal at Movenpick, which is only about two hundred yards away, and have a great evening. How about it, Fakhri?'

'All right,' Fakhri said, unwrinkling his forehead and shaking his head with a smile.

Nimal shook hands with Fakhri again and said: 'See you soon,' then went upstairs.

Padma was a bit concerned that Nimal was taking Fakhri out for a meal.

'They are very proud people. Just treat him very nicely.'

'Of course I will. I don't know what time I will be back. It's only to the Movenpick just down the road.'

'I wish you would take me there too sometimes.'

'Yes. Yes. Perhaps next week. I'll come back soon.'

Nimal rushed out of the apartment, went downstairs and rang Fakhri's bell. Fakhri came out wearing a clean white *thorbe* with a new *gutra* and a black double ring support on his head.

'Fakhri, my brother, let us go,' Nimal said, throwing his hands in the air.

Fakhri puckered his forehead again, looked at Nimal and put the two hanging ends on either side of his *gutra* over his head and checked whether the front fold of the *gutra* was in line with his nose.

They walked towards the Movenpick restaurant. 'How long you are going to stay here, Fakhri?'

'I don't know really. I want to go back to Iraq soon.'

'Why?'

'My parents and all my family are there.'

'Wouldn't you like to settle down in America?'

'Not really.'

They crossed the road and went towards the restaurant.

'Shall we sit outside or would you prefer inside?' Nimal asked.

'It is getting cooler. We will sit outside.'

Nimal pulled two chairs out, wiped the dust off using a paper serviette and sat down. Fakhri sat down and tried to adjust his *gutra*, looking at his image in the glass window.

A waiter came and gave them menus.

'They serve beautiful Scottish smoked salmon here. Would you like to try some?' Nimal asked.

'I never had that.'

'I can recommend it. The other day I brought Abdul Mubarak here, and he loved the salmon. They also bake their bread on the premises.'

'OK,' Fakhri said.

'We will start with smoked salmon, and look at the menu again. Shall we?'

'All right.'

'We can eat slowly and enjoy the meal and watch that beautiful sun in front of us going down, and forget about all the politics and the past and tomorrow as well.'

'All right,' Fakhri said, smiling.

The waiter brought the smoked salmon and the freshly baked slices of brown bread on side plates. The bread was still warm and its smell was appetising. Nimal put some butter on the bread and it was melting as he spread it. He took a bite and it tasted good. He ate some smoked salmon, and he felt happy and relaxed. Fakhri ate some smoked salmon, called the waiter and said something in Arabic. The waiter brought a bottle of Nabrasco chilli sauce, and Fakhri smothered his salmon with it and started eating it gleefully.

Chapter 12

Abdul Mubarak walked between the rows of beds. Sayeed's bed was made up with fresh sheets. Sayeed was sitting in a chair by the side of it, dressed in a clean white *thorbe* and *gutra*. When he saw Abdul he stood up and smiled.

'Kayf haalak, Sayeed?'

'Al-hamdulillah. Shukran, Abdul Mubarak,' Sayeed said. 'Inta?'

'Tayyib. May God give you health.' Abdul Mubarak hugged Sayeed and kissed both his cheeks. Nurse Nura came over to them with Sister Ulfat.

'How are we today?' asked Sister Ulfat.

Sayeed shook his head up and down with a smile and looked at Abdul Mubarak.

'Dùktoor Abdul Mubarak, he is all right to go home now. Yesterday Dùktoor Sulaiman Seif examined him thoroughly and said that it is all right. There are some tablets you have to collect from the pharmacy before you go. Sayeed, you must drink plenty of water and you must eat well to build up your strength.'

'You remember what Sister Ulfat says, Sayeed. Plenty to drink and eat,' Nurse Nura said.

'Have you got everything in that bag?' Sister Ulfat asked, pointing to the stuffed carrier bag on the floor.

'Yes, Sister,' Sayeed said.

'Off you go then. No more wandering in the desert. We don't want to get ill again, do we?' Sister Ulfat said, hands on her hips.

Sayeed smiled and picked up his carrier bag. 'Ma'a s-salaama,' he said.

'Ma'a s-salaama, Sayeed. May God give you strength,' both nurses said.

'Let me carry your bag, Sayeed,' Abdul Mubarak said.

'No. No. I am fine. Shukran, Abdul Mubarak.'

Sayeed waved to the other patients and they all wished him well. Sayeed and Abdul followed the two nurses towards the stairway down to the ground floor.

'Will you be all right walking down or shall we take the lift, Sayeed?'

'I don't need the lift. I'm not ill,' Sayeed said.

Abdul Mubarak smiled.

They walked downstairs slowly, with Sayeed holding on to the banister.

'Very hot today,' Sayeed said, coming outside and adjusting his *gutra*.

'It's been like this for a few days now. Do you want to go to the lab and see your friends before you go?'

'Not today. I'll see them soon. When I come back.'

'In that case, we will go home and see Leila. After that we'll leave for your village before it gets too late.'

'All right.'

The roads were busy with Thursday morning traffic, the beginning of the weekend, with families going on shopping trips to the *souks* in the old town or to the newly built Euromarché hypermarket on the outskirts of the city. Abdul Mubarak was blowing his horn and driving fast, sometimes blocking other drivers who wanted to overtake him.

'I think you ought to take something for little Leila. She expects sweets. Her teeth are so bad. Some are just brown stumps. I took her to see Dùktoor Ghasan at the dental school the other day. He was shocked. He said if we are not careful she'll be wearing dentures for the rest of her life.' Abdul Mubarak sighed. 'We never had this kind of problem before. They call it progress. Our children don't eat dates any more. They want foreign chocolate, and Pepsi. Kids don't drink water any more. They get too fat. Their teeth are bad. And they're always ill. Take her some fruit, some grapes or apples.'

'I don't have any money.'

'Don't worry.'

Abdul Mubarak stopped the car outside a super-market, asked Sayeed to stay in the car and went inside. He bought a few items to take to Sayeed's family as presents, some shopping for his home and some red grapes for Leila.

'You haven't seen Leila for a few weeks. She's quite

a different person. She loves going to school, and she has some new friends,' Abdul Mubarak said, getting back in the car and starting to drive.

'I hope she remembers me.'

'Of course she will. She asks about you. If she asks about Latifa, don't say anything. Not a word, please, Sayeed.'

'I have a headache. I get very bad headaches now.'

'Do you want a tablet for it?'

'No. I don't like tablets. We never used to take tablets before.'

'Your other tablets are not due yet.'

'I get these dreams. Very bad dreams. I don't remember them when I wake up but I know they're very bad and I get frightened.'

'We all get bad dreams sometimes, Sayeed. You were very ill. When you get a bit stronger you'll be all right. Don't worry, my friend. We're almost there now. You haven't been to my home before, have you?'

Abdul Mubarak stopped his car in front of his villa. He took the shopping from the back seat, and helped Sayeed out of the car. As he went through the tall metal gate he took Sayeed's hand, kicking the gate shut behind him. They climbed the steps on to the veranda.

'Welcome to my home, my friend,' Abdul Mubarak said, spreading his hands. 'Please come inside. Leila must be watching television. Let's go find her.'

'No, I'll stay here. You go in,' Sayeed said.

'It's all right, my friend. Come in, please.' Abdul took

Sayeed's hand and led him into the sitting room.

Leila and her friend Farah lay on the floor watching a dubbed cartoon. Road-Runner was charging away at full speed. They turned their heads around, looked at Abdul and Sayeed, then quickly turned back and continued watching the video, clapping hands and laughing. Then suddenly Leila stood up.

'Uncle Sayeed,' she said. She came towards him, smiling, showing all her bad teeth and throwing back her head with her two red-ribboned plaits.

'You remembered me, little one,' Sayeed said as he stroked her head.

'This is my best friend in the whole world,' she said, pointing to Farah, who was still deeply absorbed in the cartoon.

'I got some grapes for you,' Sayeed said, giving her the bag.

'I don't like grapes,' she said.

'Why not?'

'Not very tasty. I don't like their skins and the little stones. I like sweets. Have you got any?'

'No.'

'Please bring me some next time. Are you going to sleep here tonight?'

'No. Uncle Abdul is taking me to the village today. I haven't been well. I was in hospital.'

'I know. I thought you'd died.'

'Why?'

'Farah said people in hospitals die.'

'No. They stay in hospital and get better.'

'Are you better now?'

'A lot better. I'm going to the village for a rest and to get more better.'

'I like it here. I'm going to stay here. I'm waiting for Ummi. She went looking for the goats a long time ago. She must be lost in the desert. I know for sure she'll come looking for me. Were you looking for her, Uncle Sayeed?'

'Leila, go and watch television. Uncle Sayeed is very tired,' Abdul Mubarak said. 'This kid watches too much television. It's bad for their eyes. Let's go on to the veranda, Sayeed.'

'My headache is bad. Perhaps I will have one of your tablets,' Sayeed said, sitting down on the carpet on the veranda.

Abdul went inside and brought two paracetamol tablets and a glass of water and gave them to Sayeed. He swallowed the tablets, drank some water and gave the glass back to Abdul Mubarak.

'It's strange. I seem to remember Leila saying the same thing to me some time ago, that her mother went to the desert looking for the goats and was not back yet.'

'Young children make up so many stories, and they get all mixed up with the stories they watch on television,' Abdul said. 'We'd better leave soon. I'll go and see my wife. She must be upstairs.'

Sayeed slipped off his *gutra* and skullcap. He took a

handkerchief from his pocket and wiped the sweat from his head. Then he ran his hand over it. He could feel some large bald patches. Perhaps his illness had caused them, he thought. When he went back to his village he would shave it completely. He put his skullcap and *gutra* back on. Abdul Mubarak came out with Leila and her friend, and his wife with her veil down.

'Give this to your family, Sayeed,' said Fatima, giving a bag to Sayeed.

'Shukran,' Sayeed said. 'You are very kind people. You kept my family here when I was in hospital. They told me. I don't know how to repay you.'

'You are our brother. It's nothing. Don't worry about it at all,' Abdul Mubarak said. 'It's getting late. We'd better go now. Did you put in everything I need?' he asked his wife, lifting up the woman's case she had packed for him. 'I hope no one sees me carrying this.'

'Do you want me to put it in the car?' Fatima asked.

'No. It's fine. OK. We go.'

Sayeed stroked Leila's head, and kissed her cheeks. Then he stroked her friend's head, bent down and kissed her forehead. The little girls looked at each other and giggled. Sayeed smiled, waved to them and said, 'Ma'a s-salaama.'

'Ma'a s-salaama,' they replied, waving their hands. Sayeed followed Abdul down the steps and out of the gate.

'Your uncle is a very old man. I think he's going to die soon,' Farah whispered to Leila.

'No, he's not an old man. He's a very kind man,' Leila whispered back.

'Now, girls, time to do homework. Turn the television off and go to the table,' Abdul Mubarak's wife said firmly.

Chapter 13

Abdul Mubarak had been driving for more than an hour. The undulating road in front stretched all the way to the horizon, lined with fawn sand dunes with scanty parched grass and dried-up bushes and trees with only a few green leaves. The air was still under the scorching sun, and the road with its melting tar appeared to be vaporising in the distance. A few kilometres ahead a lorry, like a wavering watery image, cast dust clouds behind it. There were no vehicles coming towards them. A *masbaha* was hanging and swinging on his mirror and Abdul Mubarak could see the road and the desert all the way back to the horizon. The Chevrolet Caprice Classic glided along, locked on cruise control. It was cool inside the car.

Abdul Mubarak, myopic eyes bulging, was concentrating on the road ahead, his left elbow resting on the door, as his hand touched the steering wheel, his right hand tugging at his beard. His bare feet rested on the sandy floor. Sayeed was fast asleep, his head resting on the seat, his chin on his right shoulder. In his lap lay his skull cap and *gutra*.

Abdul Mubarak's back was very painful. He was wearing a corset, but it was still unbearable. The doctor had said that he should lie down and rest. He had a slipped disc, but he could not stop going to work, because if he stopped he would not get paid, and if that happened he would not be able to pay off the loan for his house. He wished that he had started his own business a long time ago. Some of his friends had become businessmen and they were doing very well. But he had gone to university. He had got a degree in pharmacology and a job in a laboratory. If he had started a pharmacy, his life would have been better. But hospital employees were entitled to grants for medical treatment abroad, if the local hospitals couldn't provide the required treatments.

Abdul Mubarak had asked for a grant. They had told him to apply to hospitals abroad and find out the cost of treatment. He had applied to an orthopaedic clinic in Harley Street in London and they sent him all the necessary details. He had to get several copies of this, and authorisation from several administrators, including the Dean of the Faculty of Medicine and the Director of the hospital. It was not easy to get to see these people. There was no appointment system. One just went and waited outside their offices, hoping they would turn up. That could take hours, or even days, and even then another person, a friend or a colleague, might come in and take up their time. And so it went on for another day. He still had to get a few more signatures before the final authorisation would be granted, and with his backache getting worse and with Sayeed's problems taking up his time in the last few weeks, he was beginning to get tired and short-tempered.

He pushed his *gutra* and skull cap back and scratched his head and looked at Sayeed. Still sleeping. Abdul Mubarak leaned forward and looked at the clock on the dashboard. It was past midday and he was getting hungry. The lorry in front of him was getting closer. He could see some buildings appearing before the mirage in the distance.

Abdul Mubarak loved his father, who had only married one woman, Abdul's mother. Abdul wished that he had enough money to take his father abroad for some plastic surgery. It would have been a great gift from a son to his father, to make him happy. But it was not possible for a man who had to depend on a monthly salary.

He could see the buildings ahead, on the right, clearly now. When he came closer he saw a large restaurant and a vehicle repair garage and a petrol station next to it. Some vehicles were parked in the sand. He turned right and drove among the parked lorries, throwing up clouds of dust. The shifting of the car as they left the tarred road woke Sayeed. He sat up, rubbed his eyes and squinted outside. Then he looked at Abdul Mubarak.

'Kayf haalak, Sayeed?'

'Al-hamdulillah,' Sayeed said, wiping his mouth with the back of his hand.

Abdul Mubarak stopped the car close to the main entrance of the restaurant.

'Are you hungry, Sayeed?'

'Hmmm.'

'I'm very tired. My back's killing me. The doctor said not to make any sudden movements. He said if I'm not careful I could be paralysed for life. Let's go and eat something, Sayeed. I'm famished.'

Sayeed put on his skull cap and *gutra*, opened the door and got out into the blazing heat. Abdul followed more slowly. There was a regular thumping noise coming from an electricity generator at the back of the building. Someone was hammering on metal in the garage. A small breeze disturbed the dust, stirring the plastic bags, empty cigarette packets and other rubbish that had been left lying around. Abdul Mubarak slowly climbed the steps to the main door of the restaurant, pulled it open gently and went inside, followed by Sayeed.

It was cooler inside. The restaurant was busy serving lunch to lorry drivers, almost all of the tables already occupied. Abdul Mubarak went to the refrigerator, opened the door, took out two half-bottles of water and looked around for an empty table.

A waiter came over and took them to a table where a Lebanese driver with a walrus moustache sat finishing his meal. They exchanged greetings. The driver curled his moustache, cleared his throat, took a mouthful of water from his tall glass, shook the water vigorously inside his mouth with his cheeks bulging out and the moustache trying to fly off and drank it down. He put the glass on the table, preened his moustache with both hands and rolled his eyeballs around, trying to soothe his eyes, which had been irritated by sand. Finally he wiped his eyes, then his mouth, with his serviette and got up. He smiled with his moustache ends lifted up, showing his yellowish front teeth, and said, 'Ma'a s-salaama.' Then he went away to pay the bill. Abdul Mubarak and Sayeed stood up slightly from their chairs as he left and said: 'Ma'a s-salaama.'

'This country is filling up with strange foreigners. You find them everywhere, even in the middle of nowhere,' Abdul Mubarak said, and Sayeed laughed.

Chapter 14

It was getting towards late afternoon when they approached Sayeed's village. Abdul Mubarak had been there before. He had driven Sayeed's wife back there for a visit, soon after she had first come to the city. And he had visited later with Sayeed.

Abdul left the main road and turned left onto the road that sloped down towards the village. In front of them they could see luscious green date palms swaying in a green sea with the *wadi* surrounding it and the light brown desert encircling that. They crossed the bridge over the *wadi*, turned right off the tarred road on to a rocky track and drove down to the *wadi*, which was filled with thick grey clay dust. They drove away from the middle of the *wadi* where the dust was deepest. With the tyres slipping and the bouncing front of the car spraying dust and the windscreen wipers working hard to clear the dust, and with a fog of dust behind, Abdul drove slowly with the air conditioner off.

Another driver was coming towards them through another cloud of dust. The driver slowed down when he came close, wheels skidding and spinning with the car at an angle, as he struggled to control the vehicle. When the heavy rains came in the spring, this *wadi* became a deep river with all the washed-up mud from the surrounding desert sedimenting in the middle. But when it was dry, drivers took short cuts through it, rather than using one of the bridges over it.

Sayeed was happy. He was home. He looked about to see what changes had been made since he was there last, hoping to see a familiar face, a friend or a relative.

'That's where my friend Yasser used to live,' he said, pointing to some flat-roofed mud houses on the left.

'Where is he now?'

'His parents died, so he went to the city. I haven't seen him for about thirty years. I don't know whether he's dead or alive. No one lives in that house any more. But still it belongs to Yasser.' Suddenly he sat up straighter. 'Can you stop for a moment, Abdul? I think there's a truck parked there.'

'I can't see that clearly. What do you want to do?'

'Nothing,' Sayeed said. 'It's probably just someone from the village. Young boys, maybe. Let's go. It's getting late.'

'My back is terrible. I must lie down soon,' Abdul said.

'We're almost there. After the next bridge.'

'I know. Remember once when we came here and this was flooded? We had to take the long route to get to your house.'

'When we were little, we used to swim here, Yasser

and I. Yasser was a strong boy. I wasn't a good swimmer at all. When the wadi got filled with brown water we used to tie old date palm trunks together to make a raft and pull it down here and float it on the water and row it around. It was great fun.'

'I'm a city boy. When the spring rains came the city got flooded. Sometimes the houses got flooded as well. Our shop never got flooded. We were on high ground.'

'After the rain these creatures come alive in the wadi. Some are like fish and some are like lizards with tails and some have got huge eyes and scales. They're horrible. I could never touch them. Yasser used to catch them and throw them on the sand. They jump up and down for a while and die. Some don't die easily. They wriggle for a long time. Some try to wriggle down towards the water and Yasser would kick them up in the air and the birds would catch them and swallow them. I hated those horrible creatures.'

'Now everyone driving in the wadis crushes the eggs of those creatures. They will be completely extinct one day. Those creatures survived millions of years in all kinds of weather from severe cold to extreme heat, but now we are crushing them to extinction under our tyres,' Abdul Mubarak said.

'Hmmm.'

'It is going to get dark soon, now the sun has disappeared. We are home, Sayeed.'

Abdul Mubarak turned the car to the left and climbed the steep path to Sayeed's brother's house. He parked under a tamarisk tree next to Mustafa's truck. Mustafa got up quickly from the mat on the veranda where he was sleeping, put his slippers on and came out to greet them.

'Shukran, Abdul Mubarak,' Sayeed said, opening the door.

Abdul Mubarak raised his hands above him and stretched slowly. Mustafa came around and opened Abdul Mubarak's door.

'Salaam alaykum.'

'Wa-alaykum is-salaam,' Abdul Mubarak said, slowly getting out of the car.

'Ahlan wa-sahlan,' Mustafa said, spreading his hands wide and hugging Abdul Mubarak.

'Shukran,' Abdul Mubarak said. 'I have brought your brother home as I promised.'

Mustafa went to Sayeed and hugged him tight and kissed him. Halima and Akila and the children were standing on the veranda. Sayeed looked up at them and smiled.

'How are you, brother Abdul Mubarak? Welcome to our home. Please come in. You're looking well, Sayeed. Are you going to bring our brother Abdul Mubarak in?' Halima asked.

Mustafa looked at Abdul Mubarak and smiled, and they walked on to the veranda.

Chapter 15

With a cushion behind his back and his legs stretched out on the carpet, Abdul Mubarak carefully lifted his hot cup of *gahwa* from the tray and sipped. It was dark outside. Sayeed and Mustafa sat cross-legged in front of him, drinking their *gahwa*. They were silent. The fluorescent tube above lit up the veranda and the yard outside.

Inside, the children were reciting their lessons, religious verses to be learned off pat. Halima and Akila were busy in the kitchen getting supper ready.

'Our brother Sayeed looks well,' Akila said, putting a lid on to the aluminium pot where a goat stew was simmering.

'He worries me,' Halima said. 'I don't know what to do with him. He asked Mustafa to take him to see Latifa tomorrow. Mustafa just looked at me. Then brother Abdul started to talk about something else. We can't go on like this. I don't know what is going to happen tomorrow,' she said, shaking her head.

'I'm worried too.'

'If that stew is ready, we can serve it now.'

'Ask the men whether they want their food brought out to the veranda.'

The women and children ate in the sitting room, the men on the veranda. After supper Abdul Mubarak went to Sayeed's old room to lie down. He was tired and soon fell asleep on the floor.

After the children had gone to sleep, Halima and Akila made a pot of tea with plenty of sugar, and brought it out on a tray with four small glasses. Mustafa and Sayeed were sitting quietly on the veranda with their backs against the wall. Halima put the tray down in front of them, and sat down.

'Have some nice hot tea, Sayeed. You must be very tired travelling all day,' Halima said. 'You also must be very tired. You slept all day,' she said, shaking her head at Mustafa.

Sayeed smiled.

'I have many things in my head, woman. You don't understand,' Mustafa said.

'I suppose when you sleep they all get sorted out,' Halima said, pouring tea.

They all picked up a glass of tea and started sipping it.

'I'm worried. Something is not right,' Sayeed said. 'I get very bad dreams. I know they are bad because they frighten me. When I wake up, sometimes my body starts to shake. I don't understand. Tomorrow I'm going to see Latifa. I don't remember her telling me that she wanted to go home. She would never go without Leila. Something is not right.'

'Have a good night's sleep. You'll feel better tomorrow,' Halima said.

'I'm too frightened to sleep.'

'I'm tired. I want to get some sleep,' Mustafa said, standing up and yawning. 'Why don't you get some sleep as well, Sayeed?'

'No. I am not going to sleep. And none of you is going to sleep either,' Sayeed said, pointing at Mustafa.

'Brother Sayeed, please do get some sleep. You haven't been very well and you just came out of hospital. You don't want to tire yourself, do you now?' Akila said in a soft voice.

'I'm sorry, Akila. I must know. I know you are all hiding something. Even Abdul Mubarak is hiding something.'

'Sit down, Sayeed, and calm down,' Halima said, getting up and waggling her right index finger at him, her clenched left fist on her hip.

'I am sorry, Halima, I am going to walk up to Latifa's house now. I am going to sleep there tonight.'

'You're going nowhere, I tell you. Sit down and I will tell you what you want to know,' Halima said, jabbing the air with her finger towards Sayeed's left shoulder. 'We are only trying to protect you, but I will tell you what you want to know,' she said, raising her voice.

'Please don't shout. Our brother Abdul Mubarak might wake up,' Akila said.

Sayeed slowly sat down again. Halima sat cross-legged in front of him and bent forward and wiped her forehead with the back of her hand. She sighed and looked at Mustafa and Akila and with pressed lips shook her head up and down. Then she looked at Sayeed.

'Latifa is dead, Sayeed. They buried her the other day,' she said in a soft voice. Then both the women started to cry.

Sayeed's arms dropped to his sides. He turned his head to the wall and pressed his cheek hard against it and looked to the darkness outside. 'I knew it,' he whispered with clenched teeth. 'Leila said her mother went to the desert looking for the goats. I knew it. My nightmares were real,' he whispered, with tears flowing down his cheeks. 'She will never have another glass of tea again. She will never eat another meal again. My fault. It is my entire fault. I killed her by taking her to that hellhole. It is my fault. I killed Leila's mother.' Suddenly he got up and started pacing up and down, his head bowed, whimpering and muttering, shuffling his feet and rubbing his hands on his body. Halima tried to stand up, but Akila pulled her down. They watched Sayeed pacing up and down.

'I don't know what is happening. He is muttering. Shall I wake up Abdul Mubarak? He is a dùktoor,' whispered Halima.

'No. No. Just leave him. Let him rest,' Mustafa said.

Suddenly Sayeed sat down and looked at Halima, Akila and Mustafa as if he were looking through them, and started muttering again. He quickly got up again and started to pace up and down, scuffing his feet and, with his hands crossed over his chest, rubbing his upper arms up and down. 'I will never see her again. My fault. Bad people, all of them.' He sat down again and started pulling his cheeks with both his hands, breathing fast. Then he got up and ran outside.

It was semi-dark in the palm grove. Beams of light coming from the veranda filtered through branches of bushes into the garden. Mustafa went running after Sayeed. Halima and Akila stopped him.

'Leave him alone. Don't go near him. Just watch him from a distance,' Halima said.

They stood in the dark. Sayeed was lying on the ground, his arms stretched out and his right cheek resting on the ground. Then he raised himself on one arm and started stroking the soil. 'You must be very cold down there. You should be up here. Then I could cover you with a blanket on a cold night like this. It's my fault. I'm sorry. I didn't want to get married. I am a poor man. I took you to that shanty town. You didn't like it,' he whispered, and stroked the soil gently, sharp stones and mimosa thorns piercing his flesh. Then he kissed the soil and closed his eyes.

'He's quiet now. Why don't we let him sleep there,' Halima said, wiping her eyes.

'It's very cold out there. There is a clear sky. He'll be ill again,' Mustafa said.

'If we try to bring him in, he might get violent. Best thing is to cover him up with a blanket and let him sleep. We'll have to keep an eye on him,' Akila said.

'Yes, he can be violent. Abdul told me that when they sentenced Latifa to death he started crying, and the guards came and dragged him outside and pushed him to the ground. Abdul put his hand on Sayeed's shoulder and he turned around and slapped Abdul,' Mustafa said.

'He used to be a very gentle person, but this has changed him,' Akila said.

'Then he got up and started to run. Abdul ran after him, but he couldn't keep up with him. He disappeared in the crowd. And then he was lost in the desert.'

'God guided that Bedu boy to our brother. Thank God. God is the greatest,' Akila said.

'I'll bring a mat out and watch him from a distance,' Mustafa said.

'You'll be asleep in no time. If he runs away again, we'll never find him. That'll be the end of him,' Halima said.

'I'm going to bring a packet of cigarettes and I will stay up. Have some faith in me, woman,' Mustafa said.

'I know you well enough. I am going to sit out here as well,' Halima said.

'He's quiet now. He's probably sleeping. I'll bring a blanket and make some more tea,' Akila said. 'You two must have blankets as well. It's going to be a cold night.'

Chapter 16

Mustafa and Halima sat side by side on the plastic mat, wrapped in dark brown blankets. Sayeed was sleeping on the ground, covered by the blanket Mustafa had placed over him during the night. Dewdrops had settled on it, on the plastic mat and on the grass blades where Mustafa and Halima were sitting. They were trying to sneeze quietly so that Sayeed would not wake up. The sky was getting lighter towards the east. Mustafa lit another cigarette.

'Blow that horrible smoke the other way,' Halima said.

'I always do. But it doesn't matter which way I blow it, it always comes towards your nose,' Mustafa said, laughing.

'I can't breathe with it coming towards me.'

'I've heard that some of the women in the city smoke cigarettes. Why don't you start smoking?'

'I'd rather die than be one of those modern women who smoke cigarettes and swim in pools half naked and get dressed like a dog's dinner under their abayas just to go shopping in supermarkets.'

'You have to change, woman. The whole world is changing.'

'Stop talking rubbish and think what we are going to do with him.'

'I don't know. He was always a softie. I never knew how to cope with him.'

'Why don't we send him back to the hospital with brother Abdul Mubarak?'

'The hospital did what they could. If he does not get better I am going to see Latifa's father today and ask his advice. He is a very wise man, he will tell me what to do.'

Dawn was breaking and the prayer call started from the loudhailers on the minaret of the village mosque.

'I am so cold my body is almost frozen,' Mustafa said.

'Why don't you go and pray with brother Abdul. I will keep an eye on Sayeed.'

'I am so tired. Not a wink of sleep last night,' Mustafa said, yawning.

'You were snoring. It's a good thing I stayed here to keep an eye on him. Now go and have your prayer wash.'

Mustafa stood up slowly, still with the blanket over his head. With only his face visible he slipped into his slippers and staggered towards the water tank at the back of the house. Abdul Mubarak and the boys were already there having their wash.

'Sabaah il-khayr, Mustafa,' Abdul Mubarak said.

'Sabaah in-nuwr, Abdul Mubarak. How is your back?'

'A bit better. I took some painkillers, so I managed to sleep. How is Sayeed? Is he not going to pray?'

'I will tell you about him after prayers. We haven't slept all night, Halima and I.'

'Is he all right?'

'Let's go and pray. I will tell you afterwards. He's not too bad,' Mustafa said, starting his prayer wash.

They went to the veranda with the boys and prayed there. Afterwards, Mustafa explained to Abdul Mubarak what had happened the previous night. Abdul Mubarak rushed to the palm grove where Sayeed lay, lifted the blanket up and sat beside him on the ground.

'Oh, my poor friend, what has happened to you?' he said, stroking Sayeed's head. Sayeed's tear-filled eyes were still gazing at the ground and he made no reply. 'Come, let us go in,' Abdul said, lifting Sayeed up with the help of Mustafa and carrying him to the veranda, where they sat him down against the wall. Halima brought a pot of tea and some glasses. Abdul Mubarak poured a glass and tried to give it to Sayeed, but he would not take it. He lifted the glass up and put it against Sayeed's mouth. He would not drink it. Then Halima took the glass out of Abdul's hand and told Sayeed firmly to drink it, and put it to his mouth, holding the back of his head with her other hand. Slowly Sayeed sucked a few drops until, with constant coaxing, he drank the whole glass of tea.

'I'm going to take him back with me,' Abdul Mubarak said.

'I think the hospital did what they could and they cannot do any more,' Halima said.

'I think she's right, brother Abdul, we must keep him here. We can look after him here,' Mustafa said.

'You don't understand. The hospital is the only place he can get the care he needs. I must take him with me.'

'You are a very kind man, my brother Abdul Mubarak, but I think we will keep him in the village. We can look after him.'

'Perhaps our brother Dùktoor Abdul knows what he is talking about?' Akila asked.

'No, Akila. The hospital did what it could. Now we have to take advice from our elders. We have our local remedies. I don't believe in these modern medicines anyway,' Halima said.

'I cannot force you to do anything. But if he was my own brother, I would take him to a hospital immediately,' Abdul Mubarak said, throwing his hands up in the air.

'I made some spinach soup for our brother Sayeed, shall I bring it?' Akila asked.

'Bring it with some goat stew from last night. I will feed him. I'm used to looking after children,' Halima said.

'I'll get your breakfast as well,' Akila said to Abdul Mubarak and Mustafa.

The children had fetched some fresh unleavened bread from the bakery, and Akila brought goat cheese, olives, dates and halva. While Halima fed Sayeed with slimy spinach soup, the others ate silently. The children finished quickly and went outside to play.

'Would you like some fresh goat milk, brother Abdul?' Mustafa asked.

'Boiled?'

'No.'

'I've never had it before.'

'It's good for you.'

'I usually have tea with my breakfast.'

'Milk gives you strength. You have a long drive ahead of you.'

Abdul Mubarak took a glass of goat milk, brought it about an inch closer to his eyes, fished out a floating black hair and drank it in two gulps while holding his breath.

'Would you like some more?'

'I'm terribly full up. You are most kind. I might have room for a sip of tea,' he said.

Akila poured a glass of tea and gave it to Abdul Mubarak, and he started to drink it slowly. Mustafa lit a cigarette. Sayeed was sitting with his legs stretched out and his hands on his lap, his back against the wall.

'I hope you know what you're doing. This man is very ill,' Abdul Mubarak said.

'You are most generous and kind, brother. Let me discuss this with Latifa's father,' Mustafa said.

'Can't you talk to him before I go? Or I could come with you to see him.'

'No, brother. You have to go back to the city. Don't worry.'

'In that case, I better get going.'

'I have some dates for you from our garden,' Akila said.

'Very kind.'

'I heard you couldn't get good dates in the city,' Akila said.

'They add sugar syrup to them to make them sweeter, but I think these are much tastier. They're God's fruit.' Abdul Mubarak looked down at Sayeed. 'My friend, I have to go now. You get better soon. I am coming to see you next weekend, and if you are not better by then, perhaps I will take you back to the hospital.' He held Sayeed's hand, then slowly bent forward and kissed Sayeed's cheeks and hugged him. He got up carefully. Sayeed did not respond.

'Bring him back to the hospital if he gets worse, and please take care of him,' Abdul said.

'A thousand thanks, brother. Please give our love to our sister Fatima and to our little Leila,' Akila said, giving him a plastic container full of dates.

Chapter 17

'We have become so hopeless, Mustafa,' Latifa's father Al Fawzi said with a sigh.

'I know, Uncle, it's not our fault. Wicked people did bad things to us. What can we do? Where can we go? Who would listen to us? Some of our friends in the village say that we should go and see the King and speak to him.'

'Don't waste your time, Mustafa. He doesn't want to hear from little people like us. And he's ill. I've heard that his aeroplane is a complete hospital, with modern machines and American and other foreign doctors flying with him wherever he goes. And our poor Sayeed is not well because of the injustices done to him and he cannot get help. There is no justice, Mustafa. God seems to be on their side.'

'Bad people destroyed our families, Uncle. I am sure God will punish them one day.'

'Perhaps you are right.'

'Uncle, what do you think we should do with Sayeed?'

'Don't rush into anything. Leave him for another day. You say that he is eating and drinking. Watch him carefully till the morning. He might improve, God willing. Come and see me again tomorrow. Today I am going to see the healer to ask her advice. You know Umm Abbas, don't you? She has a lifetime of experience in treating our people. People come from faraway places to get her medicine and help. She is old now, but people say she is still the best.'

'I don't know, Uncle. Do the best you can. I cannot bear to see my poor brother like this.'

'I am very happy to hear that our little princess Leila is all right. I know, son, the city killed my daughter, but I still have hope. I always believe that eventually good wins over evil. Look at Abdul Mubarak. He is the epitome of traditional Arab generosity and kindness. I wish the people who rule us were all like him, but they are a selfish bunch who are an affront to the whole Arab nation.'

'I don't know much about politics, Uncle. I am only a poor farmer.'

'You must read, son, and also speak to your elders. I wonder what Mother Salwa is doing? She went to make some coffee. You know, son, women are much tougher than us. She is coping better than me. She keeps herself very busy. We are silent most of the time. But we still talk through our minds. Every time we look at each other, or sigh, we talk. When we remember happy times we smile. We were so privileged to have such a kind daughter,' Al Fawzi said, getting up.

'Don't trouble her, Uncle. I better go back to Sayeed.'

'How can I let you go without giving you something to drink?' Al Fawzi was about to go inside when Salwa appeared, carrying a tray with a brass coffee pot and two small handleless china cups. She put it down on the carpet in front of the two men.

'Kayf haalak, Mustafa?'

'Al-hamdulillah. Shukran, Mother Salwa. Inta?'

'Tayyib,' Salwa said with a sigh. 'Poor Sayeed. It is not his fault. But how can we convince him? We are coming to see him today. We are going today, aren't we, Father?'

'Yes, yes, Mother.'

'Life must go on, Mustafa. I am glad to hear our little princess is settling down well. She is so lucky to have such good people as her adopted parents. Don't let the coffee get cold, Father. Pour a cup for Mustafa. I am going to the kitchen. Tell Halima and Akila that we are coming this evening to see Sayeed,' Salwa said, and she hurried inside.

'Yes, Mother,' Al Fawzi said. He lifted the coffee pot and poured two curves of frothy cardamom coffee into the cups.

'We have no family now, except our little princess. We are old. God will take away one of us first. I know it is a selfish thing to say, but I hope and wish it will be me first. I cannot bear to live if Mother Salwa goes first. You must promise me something, son.'

'Of course, Uncle.'

'Please look after Mother if I go first, and please help

Leila to be a very clever educated lady one day.'

'Of course I will, Uncle. Don't forget, we are your family now.'

'One good thing this ruling tribe is doing is opening up educational opportunities to women. It is good. God created men and women as equals. They must get equal chances in life.'

'Quite a long way to go for that, Uncle.'

Al Fawzi shook his head.

Chapter 18

Umm Abbas's clinic started to get busy after breakfast. Her flat-roofed mud house on the outskirts of the village basked in hot sun. Some patients with their families were sitting under the palm trees at the front of the house. Several pick-up trucks were parked nearby. The yard around the house was barren, light brown clay scattered with rubbish. An old man with a long cane squatted near the entrance. Inside, Umm Abbas was treating a two-year-old boy with pneumonia. She was completely covered with a black *abaya*, only her dust-covered wrinkled hands and the tinkling long rows of twenty-four-carat gold bangles on her forearm visible.

The little boy with drooping eyes lay, coughing and wheezing, on his father's lap. Next to them sat his *abaya*-covered mother. It was cooler inside. Umm Abbas signalled the father to undress the boy. She tapped on his head with the knuckle of her bent index finger and said: 'Hmmm,' and shook her head from side to side. The boy's parents looked at each other. Then she slapped both sides of the boy's chest and said: 'Hah.

Haahk,' and shook her head up and down. The boy started having a paroxysm of coughing.

With a smile which no one could see, she gently slapped the boy's face. His nose was forming yellow balloons of snot. She snapped her fingers at the female attendant who was crouching on the floor, covered with an *abaya*. The old woman got up with a struggle, pushed the hanging curtain across the doorway aside and went into the inner room. Umm Abbas cleared her throat, put her head out of the front door, pushed her face veil forward without lifting it up and spat on the ground. She looked around at the crowd of patients and relatives. She came back inside and stretched her hand out, gold bangles tinkling and sparkling, to the boy's father. He gave her a ten-dinar note, which she checked. She lifted her black *abaya* all the way up to her portly waist, exposing the heavily pleated long white dress with a large black floral design she wore underneath, and tucked the money into her chest.

The attendant brought a brazier full of red-hot charcoal in which an iron rod was heating. She carefully put the wooden board with the brazier on the floor and started fanning herself with her hand. Umm Abbas bent down and turned the iron rod round by its wooden handle, then got up and nodded her head to the father. He wiped the boy's nose with his *thorbe* sleeve, and grabbed his arms. The mother held the naked boy's legs as he started to struggle and cry and cough. Umm Abbas took the red-hot rod from the brazier and cauterised lines under each rib on both sides of the boy's chest while he screamed and struggled. Smoke rose from his skin and the smell of singeing flesh filled the room.

Umm Abbas dropped the iron rod into the brazier with a clatter, and a few burning pieces of charcoal and ash spilled on to the floor. She took a handful of powdered myrrh, rubbed it all over the burnt areas and said: 'Hmmm.' As the father released his hands the boy started hitting him and the father laughed. The mother wiped her tears, took the boy's little *thorbe* and started to dress him. Umm Abbas went to the front door, cleared her throat and nodded her head to the man with the cane. He pointed the cane towards one of the patients sitting with a group under the palm trees.

Towards late morning, Mustafa and Al Fawzi brought Sayeed to the clinic in Mustafa's pick-up truck. Sayeed's condition had not improved. He ate only when fed by Halima. He sat on the mat on the veranda, muttering and staring out at the yard. Because there was no improvement, Al Fawzi advised the family to bring Sayeed to Umm Abbas. Al Fawzi was an old patient of Umm Abbas and knew how good she was.

When he had become jaundiced a few years ago, she knew exactly what was wrong with him, and confirmed the diagnosis by pressing his abdomen and pummelling it. Then she cauterised the exact spot, which was tender on the abdomen over the liver, with a red-hot iron disc. His jaundice had disappeared after a few weeks. There was still a large crowd waiting, but Al Fawzi had already spoken to Umm Abbas about Sayeed. He went and told the man with a cane that they had arrived. He nodded and said Umm Abbas would see them when she had finished with her patient. When his turn came, Mustafa and Al Fawzi escorted Sayeed in, each holding one of his hands. Sayeed walked listlessly into the smoky room. They sat him down on the bench and took his *gutra* and skull cap off. Mustafa handed a ten-dinar note to Umm Abbas and she gave Al Fawzi a rusty cutthroat razor and signalled him to shave off Sayeed's hair. Sayeed did not object as Al Fawzi began. Al Fawzi kicked the falling hair under the bench, and once the head was shaved completely, he ran his hand over to check the smoothness, folded the cutthroat and gave it back to Umm Abbas. She nodded to the attendant, who brought in the brazier and a circular-ended metal rod. Umm Abbas waggled her forefinger at Al Fawzi and Mustafa, who sat either side of Sayeed holding on to his arms. Umm Abbas took the iron rod from the brazier, tapped the excess charcoal off the red-hot ring, held the wooden handle with both hands, lifted it high, placed the ring on top of Sayeed's head and held it there. Sayeed started to struggle, but Al Fawzi and Mustafa held him tight. Umm Abbas took the ring off, with some smoking burnt skin still attached to it, leaving a smouldering black circle on the top of Sayeed's head. Sayeed became unconscious. Umm Abbas threw the iron rod on to the brazier. The attendant brought a bowl of myrrh powder and Umm Abbas rubbed it on Sayeed's skull.

'He will be all right in a day or two. The blood in the head was disturbed. I put it right,' she said. 'In two days' time, if for any reason he does not improve, bring him back. Then I can fix his problem for good. If you do not bring him back, the blood may be permanently disturbed and the condition becomes irreversible,' Umm Abbas said firmly.

The attendant brought a glass of water and Umm Abbas slipped it under her veil, took a sip and drank it. Then she threw the rest of the water into Sayeed's face. He opened his eyes. Al Fawzi and Mustafa thanked her for her great professional skill and took Sayeed home.

Chapter 19

There was a slight improvement the following day. Sayeed started feeding himself. But still he was not conversing with anyone. Halima made a paste of olive oil and mixed herbs and applied it to the ring of burnt skin on his head. He winced as her callused fingers rubbed his wound.

On the next day, there was no improvement. So Al Fawzi and Mustafa decided to take him back to Umm Abbas for a second course of treatment, as she had advised. This time they took him early in the morning. It was Umm Abbas's day of teaching, and her students were getting ready for their workshops.

There were two circumcisions to perform on two little boys, each a few months old. The students checked the instrument list with Umm Abbas. A razor blade for a swift cut, an assortment of rubber rings to pull the foreskin through before the cut, a pair of scissors to tidy up, some cotton wool, and a bottle of iodine to use as antiseptic.

Umm Abbas was disappointed that her first course of treatment had not worked. Because of her long

teaching day ahead, she wanted to see to Sayeed first.
She discussed Sayeed's case with Al Fawzi and Mustafa.

'This is a simple case of disturbed blood. I thought
that I put it right with the first cauterisation. I don't
understand why he hasn't been completely cured. It's a
puzzle to me,' Umm Abbas said as she looked at Sayeed,
scratching her head over her *abaya*, and shaking her
head. 'In my opinion, there could be a trace of bad
black blood as well. I can fix it now or you can get a
second opinion from Umm Lubina in the next village.
She is one of my old students, but she gives pills and
lotions and injections like the people in hospitals. I think
someone working in a hospital trained her for that. I
stick to the traditional healing techniques, and then you
cannot go wrong. If you mix things you do not know
where you are. It's up to you. What do you want to
do?'

'Everybody says that you are the best, Umm Abbas.
Do whatever you think is right. We can see a great
improvement already.'

'Very well then. Bring the patient through,' Umm
Abbas said, walking into the anteroom. Al Fawzi and
Mustafa followed her, with Sayeed, and sat him down
on the bench inside.

'Let me have a look at your head,' Umm Abbas said,
taking the skull cap from Sayeed's head. 'Good. Very
good. Red flesh. Jolly good. You put on herbs and oil,
I see. Good. Very good. Excellent. Don't let any flies
land there. If they do, you will get maggots. Jolly good.

Excellent. Let me put something special there. Only one application is enough.' She took a dab of black arcanum paste from an old Yardley's Vaseline jar and applied it to Sayeed's wound. 'Now, Sayeed, I can see you are much better today. Ah, that's what I like to see. Smile! Carry on!' She turned back to Mustafa and Al Fawzi. 'We still have a slight problem here. Just a touch of bad black blood. I will fix it today, for good. Jolly good,' Umm Abbas said, and she put the skull cap back on Sayeed's head and snapped at her dozing attendant. Then she scratched her right temple with her forefinger. The old woman stood up slowly and went into the inner room. 'I want to borrow a gutra from one of you,' Umm Abbas said, stretching out a hand.

'Take mine,' Mustafa said, taking off his *gutra* and giving it to Umm Abbas.

The attendant brought two glasses, a piece of cloth and a cutthroat razor and handed them to Umm Abbas. She gave the *gutra* to the attendant. 'We need more light on this treatment. Bring the bench near to the door, so that I can see what I'm doing. My eyesight is not as good as it used to be, but my hands are still steady,' she said, raising a slightly shaking hand.

They sat Sayeed near the door, facing out. The attendant wrapped the *gutra* around Sayeed's neck and twisted the ends. Mustafa and Al Fawzi grabbed Sayeed's hands, as he started to struggle. The attendant started to wring the *gutra* tighter and tighter until Sayeed's face started to swell and he gasped for air.

Umm Abbas shouted at Sayeed to be still, and nodded at Mustafa and Al Fawzi. They tried to steady his head, and Umm Abbas leaned forward and cut one of the swollen veins on Sayeed's temple with the cutthroat razor. Blood started to squirt, the assistant released the twist of the *gutra* and Sayeed started to breathe faster. Umm Abbas held a glass and caught the flowing blood.

'Look at the colour of this blood. What did I say? I knew the cause. Wasn't I right? This is black blood. Bad blood. No good for him.' She collected a glassful of blood and pressed a rag on to the wound. 'I stopped as soon as the good red blood started to come,' she said. 'Now we will do the same thing to the other temple, and flush out the bad blood there, shall we?' She gave the glassful of blood to her attendant.

Sayeed started to struggle again as Umm Abbas repeated the procedure on the other side and bled another glass of blood.

'Cannot do any harm. Jolly good. So, it can only do good. Excellent. All the bad blood is gone now. You take him home now, give him a good meal. He will be good as new,' Umm Abbas said, pressing another rag on to the bleeding temple.

Sayeed was sweating profusely, and breathing fast. They took him home and left him to sleep on the veranda.

The following day, Abdul Mubarak came back. He parked the car and came and sat with Sayeed on the veranda. Mustafa and the women were very glad to see Abdul Mubarak, and Abdul Mubarak was pleased to see Sayeed looking a bit better. He hugged Sayeed and asked him how he was. Sayeed started to cry. Akila went in and made a pot of hot *gahwa* and brought it out to the veranda.

Mustafa told Abdul Mubarak about the treatment Sayeed had had, and Abdul Mubarak was angry. He remembered what a healer had done to his father's nose, how it had disfigured him for the rest of his life.

'I am a scientist and a pharmacist. I do not believe in this kind of treatment. Especially now that we have good hospitals in this country. I wish I had taken Sayeed back to the city. None of this would have happened. I feel bad.'

'Brother, I am sorry you are angry. This is our old traditional treatment. These treatments are hundreds of years old. Our people did not have modern medicine until recently, and we had no choice. We survived. So it must be good. It worked and it is still working.'

'You don't understand. I've seen so many times how these things can cause terrible complications. Hundreds of patients come to hospitals after they have been to these healers. I saw a man whose leg was cauterised too deeply. The blood supply was cut off and it became gangrenous. They had to amputate the leg to save his life. Most of these treatments work on the patient's mind, not the body.'

'Look at Sayeed.'

'Probably he would have improved anyway, if you had left him alone.'

'I'm not sure about that, brother.'

'They use kitchen knives, after using them on meat. Highly infected, or rusty instruments. The patients get septicaemia sometimes. Sometimes they cut too deep and the patient bleeds to death. They use these types of knives to cut umbilical cords as well. Babies die and mothers die too. They cauterise women for post-partum haemorrhage. Especially the Bedus when they circumcise boys, sometimes they cut more than the foreskin. Still a lot of female circumcision is carried out here. It is so cruel.'

'These are our traditions, our beliefs, brother.'

'Some traditions are not always good. We have a doctor from Sudan working at the hospital. Dr Ahamed. He was trained in public health medicine, in Edinburgh in the United Kingdom. When he finished his training he went back to Sudan and worked all over the country. What he told me was appalling. They still practise female circumcision there. Women who do these female circumcisions go from village to village carrying rusty old knives in dirty leather sheaths. They dig a hole in the ground, hold the child over it. This is a kind of female castration, and the women heal badly and are disfigured for life. He told me about a woman who was admitted to the hospital on her wedding night. The husband could not consummate the marriage because she had healed badly after her circumcision when she was a little girl. He used a knife to cut her open.'

'We don't do this to our women, Abdul Mubarak,' Mustafa said quietly.

'In some parts of our country they still do this. And another thing, you know as well as I do, our people still marry girls as soon as they reach puberty. Even royalty do this. These are just children. In other countries you go to jail for that kind of thing.'

'We cannot change our customs and traditions, brother. This is us. Our world is here. The rest of the world is another world. I am sure they have their problems too.'

Chapter 20

In the early hours of morning, the cold autumn wind was blustering down from the north. Fine sand from the surrounding desert and clay dust from the *wadi* was blowing towards the palm grove and Mustafa's house. The sound of the howling wind, lightning and thunder in the distance and the rustling noise of the palm fronds woke the animals. The goats started to bleat and move about in their pens. The chickens started squawking and the disturbed horse nearby stood up and started blowing through its nostrils.

Sayeed pulled the blanket over his head, curled up and tried to sleep. But he was cold and could not sleep. The wound on his head was almost healed now. The past few weeks had been like a nightmare. It was almost a week since Abdul Mubarak's visit. Sayeed kept saying to himself that he must get better and that he must do his duty as a stepfather to Leila, and that he wanted to get better so that he could go back to work to earn money. It was his duty too, he thought, to look after Latifa's parents now that they had no other relatives. Mustafa opened the door and came out to the veranda with a blanket over his shoulders.

'Sayeed, are you awake?'

'Hmmm.'

'It's very cold out here. Why don't you come in?'

'I'm all right,' Sayeed said in a croaky voice, pulling the blanket down and raising his head.

'The wind is very cold. You don't want to get ill again. You went through a very bad patch.'

'I'm all right. You go inside. I will try to get some sleep.'

'You can't sleep here, Sayeed. Sand and dust are blowing. You are not wearing a winter thorbe, and you've only got one blanket.'

'Just get me another blanket. I will be all right. Soon it will be day.'

Mustafa went in, brought out a blanket and covered Sayeed with it, then sat down next to him and pulled his own blanket over his head. He took out a packet of cigarettes and lit one.

'Sayeed?'

'Hmmm.'

'I'm glad you are all right now.'

'Hmmm.'

'I'm sure it was terrible for you. It was terrible for us too.' He pulled a large breath of smoke.

'Hmmm.'

'These things don't go away, Sayeed. But we must live and be strong, sometimes for the sake of others. We have to look after the women and children and our elders.'

'I couldn't look after my woman.'

'Please, we decided we would not talk about it for a while.'

'You decided.'

'Latifa's father wants to talk to you. He says, now you are better, the men must have a serious talk.'

'Hmmm. When?'

'Whenever you want. The ladies want to go for a picnic in the desert with Latifa's parents today. We must try to live, Sayeed.'

'Hmmm.'

'Oh, by the way, your old friend Yasser is back in the village.'

'Yasser?' Sayeed said, getting up and pushing the blankets aside.

'Yes. Yasser. He came to the village and came looking for you. But you were in the hospital then. He was very disappointed not to find you here. He's very tall now. Grown a very long black beard. I think he has become a mutawah. He was wearing a round turban like the people in the east of our country. He was very soft-spoken, and had a religious book in his hand.'

'Hmmm,' Sayeed said.

'He asked someone to clean up his house and went away again. But he came back the day before yesterday with a group of people. They came in big cars and they all look like mutawahs, I hear. The man they hired to clean the house and look after the place is the Yemeni tailor's brother, Ahmed. Do you remember him?'

'No.'

'Yesterday evening after work he was driving back in the wadi, back to the tailor's shop. He always stops and talk to me whenever he sees me. A good boy, Ahmed. He helps me on the farm sometimes. Very hard workers, Yemenis, and you don't have to pay them a lot either. Ahmed says Yasser's friends look like very rich people, and very educated people. They all have long beards and dress like Yasser. Most of them are young. He heard them praying and having religious discussions, and they treat Yasser with great respect.'

'Who does their cooking?'

'Ahmed. He thinks most of them are from the city. Ahmed had to buy sheep and goats to feed them.'

'I cannot imagine Yasser being a religious person. I only remember him as a boy. It has been about thirty years since I last saw him. He was my best friend, in fact my only friend. I never forgot him. Every day of my life I remembered him. There were times I was forgetting his face. Then I was sad, and there were moments I missed him so badly. I am going to see him this morning.'

'You can't go today. The women want us to go to the desert. They have already asked Al Fawzi and Salwa to come.'

'I'm going this morning,' Sayeed said firmly. 'By the time all the children and women are ready, I'll be back. I must see him today.'

'Don't be late. The women have gone to a lot of trouble.'

'Yes,' Sayeed said, pulling the blankets over his head. 'Can you take me to Yasser's place?'

'Soon after breakfast then. I'm going inside to get some sleep. Still very dark outside, but at least the wind is dying down. Looks like there's a bad winter around the corner. I will wake you when we hear the prayer call.'

'No.'

'You haven't prayed for a long time. I think you ought to start praying again soon. How about today?'

'No.'

'I'm going in. If the wind starts again, come and sleep inside.'

'No.'

'You are a very obstinate man. This is the true you. I think you're back to normal,' Mustafa said, closing the door.

Chapter 21

Halima brought a pot of sweet tea and put it down in front of Sayeed. He was sitting with a blanket over his shoulders and his back against the wall.

'I hate autumn mornings. Look at the grey sky. Depressing. It might even rain. A few months of bad weather to come, unfortunately. Last night the wind was bad. I heard Mustafa asking you to come in. You should be careful. You don't want to be ill again. Have some hot tea and warm yourself up.' Halima poured a cup of tea and gave it to Sayeed. He took the cup and started to sip. 'Where is he?'

'I think he has gone to the water tank.'

'He said you are still refusing to pray. We cannot force you to pray. We are not mutawahs. Mustafa said you are going to see Yasser this morning.'

'Yes.'

'Don't be late then. We want to go for this picnic in the desert. It will give us a break for a day. I think we ought to take some firewood and have a fire. It might be too cold out there.'

'Hmmm.'

'I remember you talking about Yasser a long time ago. You were wondering what had happened to him. He came here when you were in the hospital. Akila and I were staying at Abdul Mubarak's house at the time. Only Mustafa was here.'

'Hmmm.'

'I'm very glad your old friend is back. You have some very good friends at the hospital too, but I think the friends you make when you are little are the best. I will make breakfast. The boys have gone for bread. Have another cup of tea,' Halima said, getting up.

After breakfast, Mustafa got into the truck to drive Sayeed to Yasser's house. Sayeed came down to the yard wearing a clean white *thorbe* and *gutra*.

'Don't be late,' Halima said as he got into the truck.

'No,' Sayeed said, and shut the door.

Mustafa turned the truck and started driving along the *wadi* towards Yasser's house.

'I'm very tired. I didn't get much sleep last night,' Sayeed said.

'I asked you to come inside but you wouldn't listen.'

'I don't care about comfort any more. I have never had much anyway. I remember our father used to say: "Abstinence is good discipline." '

'They were great people, our father's generation and our grandfather's generation. They were very healthy people as well. They ate little, worked hard and were well disciplined. They were not overweight. Now we have all the comforts, and these cigarettes,' Mustafa said, taking a packet from his breast pocket and flicking it open with his thumb. He picked up a cigarette with his teeth, put the packet back in his pocket, still driving with his left hand on the steering wheel, took a lighter out of his side pocket, lit the cigarette, took a deep breath and looked at Sayeed, who was deep in thought.

'You know, I feel very nervous. Last night's lack of sleep does not help,' Sayeed said.

'He's your friend. Why should you be nervous?'

'He is a completely different person now. Not the young boy he used to be. I only know the young boy.'

'Ahk. Don't worry. You'll be all right.'

'You said he looked like a mutawah. You know I hate mutawahs now. That mutawah in the shanty town where I used to live was responsible for Latifa's death.'

'We decided not to talk about it.'

'I know. But I'm very angry and I want to talk about it. I will talk about it for the rest of my life.'

'Here we are. You can see Yasser's house now.'

'Yes,' Sayeed said, adjusting his *gutra*. 'You know, we didn't bring anything with us. How can we visit him without a present?'

'We can do that some other time, Sayeed. Just relax,' Mustafa said, turning his truck to the right, and climbing the dirt track towards the flat-roofed mud house. 'Look at all those big cars. Brand-new shiny Mercedes, Buicks and Cadillacs. Must be very rich people. I'm not coming in, Sayeed. I'll come back in about two hours to pick you up,' Mustafa said, stopping the truck.

Two men with long black beards, in white *thorbes* and round white turbans, with handguns in black gun belts around their waists, came rushing towards the truck. One stood outside Sayeed's door and the other went around to Mustafa's side. They signalled to them to open the windows. Mustafa and Sayeed looked at each other, looked at the guards outside and started to wind the windows down.

'Can we help you?' the man near Sayeed asked.

'I came to see my friend Yasser. Is he here?' Sayeed asked.

'Imam Yasser is busy. He is teaching at the moment. What's your name?' asked the guard.

'I'm an old friend. If he's busy I can come some other time. Let's go, Mustafa,' Sayeed said, looking at Mustafa.

'What is your name?' the guard enquired firmly.

'Sayeed.'

The guards walked away from the truck, whispering to each other.

'My heart is beating faster. Those men are frightening. Look at them. They have their hands on the guns. They are young people. Look at their long black beards. Let's go back, Mustafa.'

'They might shoot at us if we leave. Anyway, let me try.' Mustafa started the engine.

Both the guards came running back to the truck and signalled Mustafa to stop the engine.

'Imam is busy. Teaching. I think we know who you are. Imam told us to expect you. Ahlan wa-sahlan. Come in, friends,' the guard near Sayeed said. Sayeed looked at Mustafa.

'I'll stay with you,' Mustafa said.

'No. I want to see my friend by myself.'

'Will you be all right?'

'Of course he'll be all right,' the other guard said, and laughed.

Sayeed smiled at Mustafa, opened the door and got out. Mustafa started the truck, reversed it between two dead date palm trees, and drove it back down the track towards the *wadi*.

'Come, my friend, you are welcome to take some coffee while you're waiting,' one of the guards said, stretching his arm out to Sayeed. Sayeed followed the guards to the veranda.

'Please, my friend, gahwa?' one of the guards asked almost in a whisper. 'Imam is teaching. We will keep our voices down.'

'I drank gahwa many times with Yasser's family when I was little, sitting on this veranda,' Sayeed said, taking a sip from the handleless coffee cup.

'Yes, my friend,' one of the guards said.

'It's getting cold now, the winter is not far away,' Sayeed said. 'Soon we will have to start wearing our thick woollen thorbes.'

The guards looked at each other and smiled. 'We never wear any winter thorbes. We can bear the cold.

We can bear anything. We do not feel pain,' one of the guards said.

Sayeed swallowed a large gulp of hot *gahwa*.

'We follow our imam,' the other guard said. 'I think he's finished teaching now. I will go and inform him that you are here,' he said.

'All right,' Sayeed said, and he stood up.

Sayeed felt nervous. He tried to visualise Yasser's face, but a small boy's kept appearing in his mind. Soon after the guard left them, a tall, well-built man with a long black beard and gold-rimmed spectacles, in a white *thorbe* and a *gutra*, came out on to the veranda.

'My dear, dear brother, Sayeed, salaam alaykum,' he said, with arms open wide.

'Wa-alaykum is-salaam, Yasser, my brother,' Sayeed replied.

They hugged each other tight and kissed each other's faces with tears in their eyes, and hugged each other again.

'I have missed you,' Sayeed said, wiping his tears.

'I have missed you too, Sayeed.'

'All those years there wasn't a single day went by without my thinking of you, Yasser,' Sayeed said, shaking his head from side to side.

'Let's go into the garden,' Yasser said, taking Sayeed by the hand and leading him out. 'My parents loved this garden. You remember those jasmine bushes with their tiny dark green leaves and fragrant white flowers, and the gardenia bushes with white and light yellow flowers, and the almond trees? They're all gone. The palm trees are dead too. Everything is dead. Because there was no one to water them. But there is something here which is refusing to die, Sayeed. Come with me.' Yasser walked slowly towards the back of the house. 'There it is, Sayeed. The well. Remember? The water is still crystal clear and sweet as ever. This is what made me welcome when I came back after all those years. This sweet water.'

Yasser dropped a bucket attached to a rope into the well, and pulled it up. He put his cupped right hand in, scooped up a handful of water and drank. 'You remember the water-drinking competition, Sayeed?'

'Yes,' Sayeed said, laughing. 'We were hardly ten then.' Sayeed took some water from the bucket and drank it.

'There were those three little girls. I can't remember their names now. They were about our age. They challenged us to a water-drinking competition. I still remember that aluminium tumbler. We kept drinking and drinking. I remember my tummy was bulging like it was going to burst and I was feeling sick, and my head was spinning, but we kept drinking because those girls kept drinking as well and they were laughing at us.'

'I can't remember who won.'

'I am afraid one of those girls won, Sayeed. Sometimes they were tougher than us.'

'You were strong, Yasser. Remember the rafts we

used to build with date palm tree trunks? When it rained, the wadi got filled with brown water, and we floated our rafts downstream and paddled upstream using palm leaf stalks as oars, with the rafts going everywhere out of control.'

'Of course I do, Sayeed. You know, Sayeed, you still walk the way you used to.'

'Do I?'

'But if I met you on the street now I don't think I would recognise you.'

'I don't think I would recognise you either. We have changed a good deal, Yasser.'

'Yes. There is a good deal to change, Sayeed. I will talk to you about it later. Shall we sit down there, Sayeed, under that tamarisk tree? Somehow that survived.'

'Yes.'

'I am sorry about what happened to your wife, Sayeed.' Yasser took Sayeed's hands in his. 'Your family told me about the injustice you suffered.'

'Yes.'

'There are a lot of evil people in this world, Sayeed.'

'Yes.'

'Losing a loved one is not an evanescent pain. It is permanent. Injustice is permanent too. We will talk about that later. Tell me what you have been doing for the last thirty years, Sayeed. You are about my age, but you look older.'

'My parents died, and I had to bring Mustafa up. We did not have anyone else. So I worked on a neighbour's farm, and Mustafa came with me. That's how we lived. Now we are not too badly off. I have a good job in the city in a hospital. I'm a porter. I'm going back to work soon. What have you been doing, Yasser?'

'After my parents died, I went to live with some relatives on the east coast. They were very kind people, my uncle and aunt. Both dead now. They sent me to school, and after that they sent me to the university. I studied religion there, in a university at the west coast. I started teaching, and preaching. Most of these people here were at the same university. Some are my friends. They are from all over the country.'

A man came towards Yasser, and asked in a soft voice whether the imam and his friend would like a drink. Yasser asked the man to bring some cinnamon tea.

'I stopped drinking bottled drinks a long time ago, especially Coca Cola. It is a drink of the American infidels,' Yasser said.

'I like Coca Cola.'

'You must stop drinking it. Drink water if you need a drink, or tea,' Yasser said, laughing.

'Hmmm.'

'We are a great nation, Sayeed. We have a long history. We are a very hardy, resilient race. Yes, we belong to different tribes, and we have different customs. Even our religion is practised differently in some parts of the country. We have differences. But we have a lot more in common. Sometimes we fight each other, of course. Nothing unusual in that. It happens in every country, and is still happening, somewhere, every day. But most of the time we have lived together in harmony. This country belongs to all of us.' Yasser slapped the sand. 'Foreigners occupied this land for a very long time. They desecrated our Holy Places. But we drove them out. We did that because we became united. We were poor then. We did not have oil. We fought the Turks with swords and knives and antique guns. But still we won. My grandfather rode with that brave Englishman who fought with us. My grandfather was only a teenager then. My father said my grandfather rode all the way to the Gulf of Aqaba with the Englishman, and he could recite Arabic poetry, and could speak Arabic better than we can. He understood us. He loved our country and people, and he wanted us to be free. Sadly, my grandfather died before I was born. I would have loved to listen to his adventures. My father told me that sometimes the Englishman was so ill with fever and dysentery that people had to lift him up to mount his camel, but still he led our people.'

One of the guards brought a tray with a pot of tea and two clear glasses with pieces of cassia in them. He put a small mat in front of them and placed the tray on it and asked whether the imam would like anything else. Yasser waved his hand, and the guard went back to the veranda.

'Do you drink cinnamon tea?'

'I never had it before.'

'Have some, I'm sure you will like it.'

They took their glasses and started sipping the tea.

'We have many tribes in this country. Ajman, Murrah, Shammar, Amarat, Anazat, Harb, Mutair. It's not right that one tribe dominates this country, and calls this country by their name and calls all of us by their tribe's name. It is an affront to all the other tribes. They suppress everyone else.'

'I don't know, Yasser. I don't know much about rulers. I think they are all the same. I only care about my family and my job. It has always been hard.'

'The oil belongs to everyone, but only their tribe benefits from it. Profligacy on a scale unheard of in the history of human civilisation. Debauchery unparalleled. Bibulous kings and hundreds of their relatives pillaging our people's wealth without the slightest remorse. There are shanty towns all over the country. You lived in one. You know what it is like. When the King and his entourage go abroad, one night's hotel bill alone is sufficient to build about one hundred small houses. Our people suffer, without proper water, sanitation or health care. Oil wealth is mainly for them. The trickle of wealth they instil by building a few schools and hospitals here and there is only a minute fraction. Corruption and nepotism is rife. You don't read about that in our newspapers.'

'I can't read anyway. Sometimes it is good when you can't read. You don't have to read bad things.'

'There is no freedom. We all are born free, but we are in thrall to them from the moment we are born till we die. We read what they allow us to read. We watch the programmes they allow us to watch. They do not even allow people to bring religious books from abroad. Even books of our own religion. Only their version is allowed. We had more freedom when the Turks ruled us. People live in fear. Other sects of our religion worship in secret sometimes. They flatten their mosques, imprison them, and kill them. This cannot go on for ever. It must stop, and we are going to stop it. The main reason for these degradations is because we are deviating from the fundamentals of our religion. Religion cannot be changed with time and if it does it will not be the same religion,' Yasser said, raising his voice and shaking his clenched fists.

'I can't believe that you have become so religious, Yasser. Are you married?'

'No, none of us are married. We do not need attachments. We have a mission. I am afraid, even with you, Sayeed, I am not at liberty to discuss what we are doing.'

'You are a clever person, Yasser, I am sure you will do the right thing.'

'You suffered because of this system. It was responsible for the injustice you suffered. The mutawahs are on the government's payroll. Most of them are corrupt. You must seek justice for yourself, Sayeed. It is the only way.'

'I know it was injustice, Yasser, and I am very angry with all those people in the shanty town who gave wrong evidence against my wife and got her killed. I want to kill them all. For the last few nights I have not been able to sleep. I wake up and shake with anger and I want to see their blood. I do not care what happens to me.'

'You must take revenge, Sayeed. You must take revenge,' Yasser said, raising his voice. 'A wound for a wound, Sayeed. Nose for a nose, ear for an ear. A tooth for a tooth, Sayeed, an eye for an eye,' Yasser shouted, shaking his fists. 'These are God's own words.' The followers walking in the garden looked at them.

'My grandfather's dagger was given to me by my father. My grandfather slew many Turks with it. It is curved like a hawk's beak, with this you can eviscerate your enemy. I take it wherever I go. It is very precious to me.' Yasser took an old decorated leather sheath from his side pocket. 'I am going to give it to you because you are my best friend. I want you to redress the injustice done to your wife, Sayeed. An eye for an eye, Sayeed,' Yasser shouted, holding the dagger high, clenched in his fist, and shaking his arm. Then he put the dagger in Sayeed's hand.

Chapter 22

'I didn't ask for this fate, Yasser. I didn't even want to get married. All that was imposed on me. But because of me, an innocent person was abused, tortured and died. I need their blood, Yasser. They shed her blood and I will shed theirs.'

'My brother Sayeed, please do not tell a single soul about this and do not let anyone see the dagger. You have your mission and we have ours. We will cleanse this land with blood, Sayeed. Justice is on our side. I would like to go inside now, Sayeed, and teach for about an hour before the prayer time,' Yasser said, standing up and shaking the sand off his *thorbe*. 'Some of my followers are from very rich families. Al Qusaibis. Bin Ladens. Al Amoudis. Baroums. Binzagrs. We have at least one follower from each tribe, but no one from the ruling family. Do not discuss anything we talked about with anyone. May God be with you, my dear brother.' Yasser hugged Sayeed and kissed both his cheeks. 'It gives a wrench to my heart to say goodbye, Sayeed. If we do not see each other again, please remember the love and affection of our friendship and we will meet again in heaven.'

'May God go with you, Yasser.'

Yasser held Sayeed's hand and they walked slowly to the front of the house.

'My brother is waiting in the truck to take me home. InshaaLLa, see you soon, Yasser.'

'InshaaLLa, my brother Sayeed. InshaaLLa.'

They hugged each other again, and looked at each other's moist eyes, shook their heads and walked away in opposite directions.

'I feel very sad,' Sayeed said, getting into his seat and shutting the door.

'He has become too religious. I don't think I like him very much,' Mustafa said, turning the truck towards the *wadi*.

'Leaving good friends brings sadness.'

'Associating with bad people bring sadness too.'

'That's a different kind of sadness.'

'We are already late. The women will be furious. We will have another kind of sadness soon if we don't hurry up,' Mustafa said, lighting a cigarette.

'I'm going back to work soon,' Sayeed said.

'Why? Are you sure that you are fit enough to go back?'

'Of course I am. I have to start earning money. I still owe the hospital money.'

'The money you borrowed for Latifa's dowry?'

'Yes.'

'Hmmm. You never listened to me anyway. If you

must go back I will drive you down there.'

'No. I will catch a minibus or a truck. I will go back on my own.'

'Stubborn man. Where are you going to stay?'

'I don't know yet. But I will find somewhere. It is not a problem.'

'We will have to forget the past and get on with the future.'

'Not yet.'

'What do you mean?'

'Not yet.'

'You sound strange.' Mustafa turned the truck towards the house.

'Al Fawzi and Salwa must be here,' Mustafa said, pointing to the truck parked in front. 'Halima is there. Gawd bless her. Look at the fury on her fat face,' he said, stopping the truck. 'You get out first, Sayeed. She will not shout at you. You haven't been well.'

'I am sure she is not going to shout. We aren't that late.'

Mustafa got out and kicked the truck. 'Kept stopping. I don't know what's the matter with this scrapheap. High time I went to the auction and got another Sierra.'

'Your hands are clean. You can't even lie properly. Get these things loaded up. We are late already, and we have kept our guests waiting. The children will be asking for food soon. There is some firewood to take as well,' Halima said.

'Salaam alaykum, Al Fawzi, Salwa. I am sorry we kept you waiting.'

'Wa-alaykum is-salaam. Don't worry. We had some tea while we were waiting,' Al Fawzi said.

'Sayeed has not seen his friend Yasser for thirty years. Our visit took a little longer than we thought,' Mustafa said. 'I had better load the truck up. The women are getting impatient.'

'How are you, Sayeed? You are looking well,' Al Fawzi said, getting up and hugging Sayeed.

'I am very well. Going back to work in a day or two.'

'Yes?'

'Yes.'

'We better get ready, Salwa. Go and help Halima and Akila. I will help the men.'

Mustafa followed Al Fawzi's truck and they drove slowly on the rugged desert tracks for about five kilometres until they reached the mountainous area with escarpments with fallen-down boulders at the base. A meandering *wadi* ran in the valley between the hills and mountains. They followed the *wadi* until it disappeared behind a bluff. They stopped by a thorny tree with scanty leaves by the bank, got out of the trucks and started to unload.

'Why are you looking so sullen, Sayeed?' Mustafa asked as he unrolled a green plastic mat for them to sit on. Sayeed scowled back. 'You are a sage, Al Fawzi. Tell me, now he is well, why is my brother becoming unwieldy?' Al Fawzi smiled and put down the large container of rice Salwa had made that morning and started tugging his beard with his right hand.

'Leave him alone, Mustafa,' Halima said. 'Remember, he is your older brother. He has not been very well. If you are in a bullying mood, just shut up. Unload this wood and build a fire over there. Even though the sun is out, it is still cold.' She picked some wood from the back of the truck and threw it on the ground.

'The wind is chilly,' Salwa said. She stood near the back of the truck, trying to lift down a basin of cooked goat meat. A skinned head lay on top, with grinning teeth and eyes still in their sockets.

'Children, don't go far away, and wear your slippers. The stones are very sharp,' Akila said, helping her young daughter to put on a coat.

Halima brought over a large flower-patterned vacuum flask and put it on the mat. 'Salwa, please give Al Fawzi some tea. I will get some cups.' She walked back to the truck.

Al Fawzi sat on the mat, Mustafa and Sayeed next to him. 'Sit on these. The rocks are hard,' Akila said, bringing some red cushions. Halima brought the cups and set them down. 'Mustafa, light that fire.'

'I need a cigarette and a cup of tea first,' Mustafa said, twisting the ends of his moustache and laughing, showing his brown teeth.

Al Fawzi pumped out a cup of tea and gave it to Sayeed. 'Ashkurak,' Sayeed said, taking the hot cup in both hands. Mustafa lit a cigarette, inhaled the smoke, held it in his lungs and let it out slowly through his nose. 'Ashkurak,' he said, as Al Fawzi handed a cup to him. Al Fawzi pumped another cup. 'Mother, drink this and warm yourself. Ladies, come and sit down and have some tea before you get the food ready.'

'Let's go and have some tea,' Halima said to Salwa and Akila. They sat down facing the men. Halima lifted her head and watched the children trying to climb down the slope into the *wadi*. 'Be careful on the bank. Don't fall down. Go down slowly,' she said.

Akila's daughter reached the bottom first and started walking on the circular convolutions of the large fossilised ammonite in the middle of the *wadi*, and the other children followed her. Around them large fossilised tree stumps of different heights were scattered like stone steps to the past. The children started picking up stones and fossilised shells and throwing them down the *wadi*, trying to hit a thorny bush.

'We have all had a very bad time recently,' Al Fawzi began. 'But we cannot moan for the rest of our lives.' The others looked at him, in silence. 'Sayeed says that he is going back to the city. That is good. Go back, son. God will give you strength. You will be all right. I'm so glad for our little princess, Leila. She is settling down well, we hear. Salwa and I will visit her soon. I'm glad she's going to school. Even though our deposed King Salim was so wasteful, he did one good thing. He built universities for women. Now we have women teachers, doctors, scientists and nurses.'

'Is anyone hungry?' Halima asked.

'I can wait a bit longer,' Al Fawzi said.
'Start that fire, Mustafa. We are getting cold.'
'InshaaLLa.'
'I mean now.'
'Let's start the fire, Mustafa,' Sayeed said.

Chapter 23

All the way back to the city from the village, Sayeed was thinking. He knew that he had to do it in an effective and efficient way. The *mutawah* was bigger and stronger than Sayeed. Also, people would try to stop him. The best way was to attack in the night under cover of darkness, after the last prayer of the evening, when everyone was inside their huts. That way he could make a swift kill, and run away quickly. If he could get away quietly, he could escape the police and then justice would be done. Yasser's words kept echoing in his mind: 'Redress the injustice done to your wife.'

He felt for the dagger in its leather sheath inside his side pocket, and squeezed the handle hard. A few passengers were asleep, but the minibus driver, with his red-and-white-chequered *gutra* ends floating behind him, a toothbrush stick in the corner of his mouth, was pressing the horn and trying to overtake a tanker. Dust started to fly, when finally they left the road and drove very fast on the outside to cut in front, then sped off along the tarred road. The sleeping passengers were woken by the commotion and held on to their seats. It was late afternoon and they were approaching the outskirts of the city.

When they arrived at the terminus, Sayeed got into the cool autumn air of the city. The streetlights were already switched on. Arabic music was playing loud in the neon-lit shops. He started to walk fast towards the airport road and the hospital. The roads were busy with evening traffic, the air filled with exhaust fumes and dust. Overcrowded minibuses sped past, tilting over as passengers hung on, legs dangling from the bus door. Yellow taxis zigzagged through the crush, horns blaring and music playing.

Sayeed wore his grey woollen *thorbe*, and carried two plastic bags, one filled with his clean clothes and the other with some dates from his garden for his friends in the laboratory. He walked quickly along the airport road, came to the entrance to the hospital and entered the lab through the side door. Hameed was putting his washed underwear on a line in the corner of the biochemistry department when he saw Sayeed coming in.

'Sayeed, my friend, you are back. Salaam alaykum.'
'Wa-alaykum is-salaam.'
'Kayf Haalak?'
'Tayyib.'
'Inta?'
'Quaish. Habibi.'
They hugged and kissed, and Hameed took Sayeed into the sitting room.

'Sit down, Sayeed. You must be tired. Would you like some tea?'

'Yes. Thank you.' Sayeed put his bags down on one chair and sat in the one next to it. 'Where is everyone?'

'They've all gone home. Only the on-call staff are on duty now. Dr Salim was here a little while ago. The clinics are not very busy this evening.'

'Abdul Mubarak?'

'Home. It is almost half past six now. It is good to see you looking well, my friend. Welcome home.'

'Thank you, Hameed. Nice to be back.'

Sayeed spent the night in the laboratory, sleeping on a couple of chairs in the sitting room. Hameed slept next to him. During the night, Sayeed woke up. The fluorescent tubes above were turned off but the lights in the haematology department were on. He could hear a centrifuge running and the scuffing noise of the haematology technician's slippers. Light filtered through the glass partition into the sitting room. He could see Hameed asleep in the chair with his legs over the backrest of the chair in front. Sayeed pushed his chair forward slowly, and without putting his slippers on, quietly left the sitting room. He crept through the next room, which was in darkness, and through the side door to the outside.

It was cold but quiet outside. He walked to the front of the hospital, feeling the fine grains of sand under his feet, and sat on the cement wall of the defunct water fountain. He looked up at the staff residential building –

some of the windows were still lit – and at the mosque beside it. He was pleased to be back at work and to be with his friends, but at the same time he was frightened. The nightmare which had awoken him a few minutes before played over in his mind. He was trying to attack the *mutawah* in the shanty town, but the *mutawah* had somehow managed to grab the dagger Yasser had given him and was holding it at Sayeed's throat as he woke up. Sayeed got off the cement wall and walked around the laboratory building. He went back in quietly and drank some water from a tap in the biochemistry department, then went back to the sitting room and tried to sleep again.

The loudhailer started to broadcast the early morning prayer call. Sayeed opened his eyes. Hameed was fast asleep, and the haematology department and the sitting room were quiet and dark. The hum of a refrigerator broke the silence. Sayeed slowly pushed his front chair forward, slipped his feet into his slippers, put his skull cap and chequered *gutra* on, and tiptoed out of the sitting room. Outside, morning was breaking. He came out on to the side road of the hospital. A few cars were driving along, headlamps on, towards the airport road. Sayeed walked past the nurses' home and past Dr Abdullah's stationery shop and the women's dress shop. A long bridal dress hung in a glass case lit with four fluorescent lights. He passed the grocery shop, its corrugated shutters still down.

He walked fast, adjusting his *gutra* so that its ends protected his ears from the autumn wind. The lights were turned off at the hospital switchboard. The Egyptian manning it lay fast asleep on the floor on his plastic mat. Sayeed turned right at the crossroads and walked towards the Movenpick restaurant. The waste ground to his left was full of parked vehicles. Sayeed walked fast, feeling freshness in the morning air, and turned right at the deserted restaurant. He walked past a battered burgundy Pontiac, black vinyl peeling off its roof, and towards the airport road. The dual carriageway was already busy.

Sayeed was sweating now in his woollen *thorbe*. He walked past the main entrance to the hospital and past the wall of the Al Mayamah hotel. He came at last to the next crossroads and turned right and walked towards Sara Sitteen. It was getting lighter, but out on the dual carriageway the cars' headlamps were still lit.

He was back at work, but he had no home to go to. His wife was dead and her daughter lived now with Abdul Mubarak. Sayeed felt very lonely. He walked fast, with the ends of his slippers slapping his soles with every step. He put his hands into the side pockets of his *thorbe* and felt the handle of the dagger and gripped it tight. He pulled his hand out and wiped the sweat from his palm on his *gutra*, then turned around and started to walk back towards the hospital.

In the sitting room, Hameed was having a glass of tea after his prayers. Sayeed made himself a glass of tea and sat down next to him.

All Sayeed's friends and colleagues were glad to see him back at work. Abdul Mubarak told him how well little Leila was settling down. His back was still extremely painful, and he was still collecting signatures for his surgery in London. He told Sayeed that he was hoping to take his wife and Leila to England with him. His father was going to give him some money for expenses. He was wincing with pain, slowly stretching to ease his back. He said that in other countries people did not have to work when they were ill. But if he did not come to work there was no salary.

Finding accommodation for Sayeed was a problem. Hameed suggested Abdul Mubarak should ask the cleaning company Hameed worked for to give Sayeed a bed in one of their accommodation blocks in the Al Barra area. Hameed himself shared a room with some Bangladeshi, Pakistani and Sri Lankan workers. Abdul Mubarak agreed to ask the company.

The accommodation was for company employees only, but Abdul Mubarak was persuasive. He mentioned the name of the hospital director and hinted that he had influence with him. But the only way Sayeed could get accommodation in the cleaning company's block of flats was as an employee. So the manager gave him a part-time job as a cleaner in the kitchen. Sayeed had to clean it in the evening after the cleaning staff's meals were cooked and served. Instead of wages he was given a bunk bed in a room with seven Pakistani workers. There was a malodorous en-suite bathroom with a squatter toilet, which had not been cleaned since it was built. A leaky brown sink with one cold tap stood in a corner and a dripping metal shower was fixed on to the wall nearby.

When Sayeed went to see his new accommodation he was overjoyed. A bed to sleep in and all the modern comforts to go with it was very pleasing. He pressed the mattress of his bunk with the tips of his fingers and felt the firmness. Then he lay down, put his hands under his head on the foam pillow and looked at the double metal sliding window with its fly-proof screen. He moved in on the same day. When his roommates came back in the evening after work, Sayeed tried to communicate in sign language. His roommates were a little cautious at first, in case he might spot a difference between the ordinary cigarettes they smoked and hashish. But they soon realised that Sayeed was a simple local who knew little of worldly vices, and that he was not a spy either.

Sayeed got used to a routine: finishing work at the hospital and staying on in the laboratory till about seven thirty, then walking back to Al Barra to eat the left-over food the cook kept for him, cleaning the kitchen floor, emptying all the bins and walking up to the fourth floor to sleep on his bunk.

Abdul Mubarak took him to his home after work one day. Sayeed was very glad to see Leila reading her books. Abdul Mubarak's wife was teaching her, and she was repeating religious verses off pat. Leila showed Sayeed her arithmetic and English books and read a nursery rhyme in English. Leila asked Sayeed whether he had found her mother, but he shook his head and looked away. After the meal, Abdul drove Sayeed back to Al Barra.

He woke up in the middle of the night, in the dark. He took his dagger from underneath his pillow, slipped it out of the sheath and felt the sharpness of the point on his palm for a moment, then put it back in the sheath and tucked it under the pillow. He tried to sleep, but the anger within him was getting stronger. His stomach was growling and he was thirsty. He did not want to get up in case the noise woke the others. He turned towards the wall.

When he woke up again, the anger was still there, so was the tiredness.

The following day after work, he caught a minibus from the airport road and headed for the shanty town. About half a kilometre from his home, he got out and started to walk. When he came to the outskirts of the shanty town, he suddenly lost courage and turned back and caught the minibus back to Al Barra. That night he had no appetite for food. He cleaned the kitchen the way they had instructed him to do, then went to his bunk bed and fell asleep.

The following morning Sayeed went to work as usual, and was having his glass of tea in the sitting room with Hameed and Abdul Mubarak when George Fielding and Nimal came rushing in. Full of excitement, Nimal asked Abdul Mubarak whether he had heard the news.

'No, what's the matter?' Abdul Mubarak asked, alarmed.

'Some terrorist group have taken over the Great Mosque. They've got hostages and they've already killed lots of people.'

'Don't talk rubbish. That does not happen here. You will get into trouble, talking like that. Be careful,' Abdul Mubarak warned, getting out of his chair with a struggle and putting down his glass of tea on the table.

'I heard it on the BBC World Service. It's very reliable. They would not say it unless they were absolutely sure.'

'Rubbish. This is Western propaganda. They're trying to ruin the reputation of this country and trying to insult our religion. Too much American and Western influence in this country. We want them out of here!' Abdul Mubarak yelled, pointing his finger at Nimal.

George Fielding whispered something in Nimal's ear.

'There's no need to whisper. There are no terrorists in this country. This is a peaceful country. Now, go and do some work. Don't let Mohammed Sofail hear about this. He's a very religious man. He'll call the religious police straight away,' Abdul Mubarak shouted.

'Let's go, son. He'll find out soon enough,' George said to Nimal, and they left the sitting room.

It was only in the afternoon that official news started to trickle out. A group of about three hundred armed men had entered the mosque, taken over the minarets, and held the imam at the microphone at gunpoint. They had hoped to find the King and his family present, but when they discovered his absence they realised the futility of their mission. The rebels, religious fundamentalists opposed to the ruling regime, had withdrawn to the basement of the mosque with their hostages and prepared for a siege.

All afternoon there was speculation and rumour, some of it spread by the foreign workers who had listened to American and British radio stations. The rebels had come prepared, with sacks of dates and rice as well as Kalashnikovs. Rioting had broken out in the eastern province in support of the fundamentalists, but it had been quickly and ruthlessly subdued.

Abdul Mubarak sat in the sitting room silently comforting himself with a hot glass of tea.

Two weeks later, the siege was over. The surviving rebels had surrendered. They were tried by the religious court and sentenced to death by beheading.

Abdul Mubarak came to work the day after the executions with a rolled-up newspaper under his arm. He went to Sayeed, put his arm around his shoulders and took him to the sitting room. He made Sayeed sit down and sat next to him.

'How are you, Sayeed?'

'Fine, Abdul Mubarak, and you?'

'Still in pain. And I still haven't got all the signatures

I need for permission to go to England. My friend, I have some very bad news for you.'

'What?'

'I have read in the newspaper the names of those who were executed, the rebels who desecrated the Great Mosque. Your friend Yasser Al Rasheed was among them. They beheaded him yesterday.'

Chapter 24

Sayeed bent forward and put his hands on his forehead and closed his eyes. He knew Yasser had become very religious, but never thought that he would challenge the King and the government. Whatever his politics or whatever he had done, he was still Sayeed's dear friend from childhood. Sayeed felt Yasser was wrong to kill all those innocent people in the Great Mosque and desecrate the Holy Place. He did not feel bitter against the government for punishing Yasser, but he felt great sadness at his horrific death. He would have given his life to protect Yasser, and he knew that Yasser would have done the same for him.

Memories kept coming into his mind: Yasser as a little boy, then as a teenager, and after all those years of absence his appearance as a grown-up man with a long beard. He remembered Yasser's last words to him: 'It gives a wrench to my heart to say goodbye, Sayeed. If we do not see each other again, please remember the love and affection of our friendship and we will meet again in heaven.'

Sayeed sighed and sat up straight and wiped his tears

with the end of his *gutra*. He looked at Abdul Mubarak sitting next to him. Abdul shook his head and held Sayeed's hand.

'You don't have to work today. I will tell Dr Salim. If you want to go back to your room, please go.'

'I think I will stay. At least I have some people here to talk to. Those Pakistanis do not speak Arabic.'

'I hear the King is critically ill now. It is not in the newspapers, but I heard it from a doctor friend of mine. They have a fully equipped intensive care unit inside the palace. He had several heart attacks before, but my friend says he is in a coma now. Don't tell this to anyone. No one is supposed to know. Perhaps the thought of being taken hostage made the King have a heart attack. Only I know Yasser was your friend. Don't tell anyone. If the authorities knew this they might take you away. They're very paranoid at the moment. Well, they are always paranoid. But their luck has not run out yet. In some ways the rebels were right. Don't tell anyone that I said that.'

'Yasser was more than a friend to me. He was like a brother. All my life is engulfed in sadness, Abdul Mubarak. Sometimes I cannot remember happiness.'

'My dear friend, when you wake up in the morning and look outside, and when you hear the birds singing, and see trees laden with fruit and plants covered with flowers, or the beautiful sky glowing orange with the rising sun, you see the beauty of what God created. That is happiness. You don't need people to make you happy.'

'Perhaps you're right, Abdul Mubarak. But none of that can replace what I have lost.'

'Given time, you will heal, my friend. That's how it is with everyone. I better go and do some work. What are you going to do?'

'I think I will go for a walk.'

'All right. Don't go too far. You haven't been well recently,' Abdul Mubarak said, getting up from his chair.

When Sayeed came out of the hospital, he saw lorries full of soldiers, battle tank carriers with tanks on board and armoured personnel carriers heading towards the airport. All along the road, on both sides, there were soldiers with machine guns. Sayeed felt a bit apprehensive. He decided to turn off the main road and began to walk down a side road. He stopped at a small cafeteria, ordered a kebab roll and a glass of tea and sat at a table inside. He ate slowly. The radio was loud, he did not hear it. Today is the day, he thought, that the *mutawah* must be recompensed. No time to lose. The King was ill, but justice must be done. That was Sayeed's duty as a husband. That was his responsibility. It was everyone's wish. His forefathers, the Al Rasheeds, would have done the same, only they would not have delayed so long. He must not humiliate their name by being a coward and ignoring the honour of his family and his ancestors. Sayeed drank the last drop of tea from his glass, paid the waiter in the empty café and walked out into the mild autumn sun.

He had to be alone. He decided to go to Al Barra and stay there until nightfall. The Pakistanis were at work and the room was empty. He took his *gutra* off, and lay on top of the bed and closed his eyes. But his mind was restless. He got up and went down to the kitchen in the basement.

The chef was preparing lunch. He asked Sayeed whether he wanted any and Sayeed said yes, and started to help the chef with his work. Back home Sayeed did not have to do any kitchen work. Only the women worked in the kitchen. But in the city, men had to do women's work as well. He enjoyed helping the Pakistani chef, and listening to his broken Arabic. The chef, sweating profusely, would stop now and then and wipe the sweat from his bare upper body and head with the kitchen towel. Then he would blow his nose and with the towel on his shoulder lean back against the wall and move up and down to scratch his back.

Then he would roll one of his special cigarettes, light it and pull a very long breath of smoke, then stand motionless and hold the smoke with his eyes widening and his face getting red. Once the smoke worked on his body he would dance all round the kitchen with his hands curling away like the smoke, gyrating his body like a Pakistani film star, singing Urdu love songs which Sayeed did not understand.

Beating the kitchen worktop like a *tabla*, he would sing a long note with his head thrown back and his left hand on his heart, his right hand stretched out towards

Sayeed. Sayeed was greatly amused by the chef's performance.

After lunch, he went back to his room and tried to sleep, but lay thinking. He took out Yasser's dagger and pulled it out of the sheath. He felt the sharp point on his left palm and kissed it. He turned around and cut a line on the wall. Plaster dust fell on the mattress. He wiped the blade and put the dagger back in its sheath and blew the dust off the mattress.

When he woke it was night. The room was still empty. He could see the city lights through the window. He could hear the call for the evening prayer. He wanted to be in the shanty town just after the last prayer of the day. If he started soon he might get there on time.

He put on his skull cap and *gutra*, checked his money and the dagger in his pocket, and left. The streets were almost empty. Most of the men were either praying or inside, drinking tea and smoking cigarettes far from *mutawahs*. The bus terminus was deserted.

After prayers, the city came to life again. Sayeed sat on the back seat of the bus. There were barriers across the airport road and soldiers with machine guns standing around. Traffic was building up, the passengers were whispering and angry drivers were blowing their horns. The minibus driver drove along side roads towards Sara Sitteen and from there he joined the wide road leaving the city.

Sayeed sat on his own. The driver was playing Arabic

music on his cassette player, swaying to the rhythm like a metronome. Sayeed could feel his heart beating faster.

The bus left the city and drove along the main road to the east. When it came to the turning to the National Guard primary care unit, Sayeed got up and asked the driver to stop. He got off in the dark and the minibus drove off. All around him was desert. He could see the lights of the city far away to his right. About two kilometres away in front of him on the other side of the care unit he could see the scattered lights of the shanty town.

He crossed the road and started to follow the new road. The pylons ran parallel to the road and the overhanging electricity cables were swinging in the air. Even with the autumn breeze blowing, Sayeed felt warm, and he started to sweat. He kept seeing Latifa's face, her innocent smile. 'I will avenge your death,' he screamed. The empty desert absorbed his words. His heart was pounding away and he felt as if he was floating above the ground.

He started to run, with sweat pouring from him, and he shouted: 'I am coming, you devil, mutawah, be prepared, I am coming. You killed my wife and you will be dead soon.' He took the dagger out of the sheath and started to stab the air as if in a frenzy. He started to run faster with his dagger stabbing the air. 'Oh, Latifa, please forgive me. I became the death of you. Oh, sweet Latifa, forgive me. I will take revenge for your death. For your death.'

He did not want any of the guards at the primary care unit to see him, so he left the road, crossed under a line of overhanging electricity cables and started to walk on the rugged desert. He remembered Yasser's words: 'You must take revenge, Sayeed. You must take revenge. A wound for a wound. Nose for a nose, ear for an ear. A tooth for a tooth, an eye for an eye.'

'Life for a life,' he said. 'For your life, Latifa, that animal's life.' Already he could hear the noise of television and music coming from the shanty town. He slowed down a little and started to get cautious. He did not want anyone to see him.

He left the dust track and decided to walk around the shanty town and come up behind the *mutawah's* hut. He took off his *gutra* and his white skull cap and put them in his left pocket. He was near his old hut. He wanted to see whether anyone was living there. It was empty. He remembered how he had built it with the help of his friend Hussein Hasmi. The animal pen and the toilet he had built were gone, and the roof of the hut was damaged. He came up and touched the corrugated iron of the roof. He tried to visualise Leila playing on the sand outside and Latifa sitting inside the hut. He wiped his tears and started to move away very slowly. He did not want to disturb the goats. If they started bleating, people would come out.

Now he could see the *mutawah's* big hut. He walked slowly, looking all around, and came and squatted quietly behind the *mutawah's* hut. He could smell the food being cooked inside. He could hear the cooking pots being moved around and the *mutawah*'s voice, reading aloud. Sayeed wiped his right hand on the soil, rubbed his fingers on his palm and took the dagger out. He gripped the handle tight and stood up. 'Life for a life, life for a life,' he whispered. 'An eye for an eye, and for your life, Latifa, his life now.'

He bent down, picked up a stone and threw it at the front of the house. It did not make a noise. So he picked up another and threw it at the metal barrel near the front of the hut. He heard someone coming out. Light spilled out of the hut and fell on to the front yard. Sayeed saw the *mutawah* come out. He raised his hand with the dagger and was about to charge when a little girl came running out behind him. Sayeed could see the ageing *mutawah*'s face and his grey beard and his red-and-white-chequered *gutra*.

'Why you came out, abu?' the little girl asked.

'I thought I heard a noise.'

'It must be a goat, abu. Please come back in and read the story for me.'

'I cannot see any goats, my princess. You go in,' the *mutawah* said, looking around.

'They must have gone away, abu. Please come in. I want to know what is going to happen to that little boy and girl in the story who got lost in the desert.' The little girl started pulling her father's hand.

The *mutawah* slowly followed the little girl back inside and shut the door. Sayeed stood there as if frozen.

Sayeed put the dagger back in his pocket and walked away slowly from the shanty town with his head bowed. He followed the electricity pylons and walked towards the main road. He passed the care unit and stopped in between two pylons, took out his dagger and started to dig a hole. He cut the soil with the dagger and with his hands scooped out earth. When the hole was about two feet deep, he dropped the dagger into it and spread the earth over it. He stood up, stamped the top with his slippers, smoothed it over and spread some topsoil.

All around him was the dark desert and under his feet and under the soil was the dagger. He walked away slowly, slapping his hands together to shake off the soil. He took his skull cap and *gutra* out of his pocket and put them on. He walked on to the main road and caught a minibus back to the city. From the bus terminus he walked back to the hospital and went into the laboratory.

'Sayeed, where were you? Abdul Mubarak said you went for a walk and never came back. The army is everywhere. We were worried. Did you hear the King died this evening?'

'No.'

'The television was broadcasting prayers all evening.'

'Yes.'

'You look better, Sayeed.'

'Yes. I am happy.'

Chapter 25

When Sayeed woke up it was in the early hours of the morning. He had cramps in his legs and he slowly pushed the front chair forward and started rubbing them. Hameed was still asleep and the sitting room was dark. Sayeed smiled and whispered, 'Latifa, I forgave them all.'

The early morning prayer call started broadcasting from the loudhailers on the hospital mosque. He closed his eyes and repeated the call. Hameed woke up and started rubbing his eyes.

'Sayeed?'

'Yes.'

'Let us go and pray.'

'Yes.'

Sayeed prayed and asked God's forgiveness for not praying for a while and for having evil thoughts. He promised that he would never hate anyone again. He came out of the mosque and looked up at the rising sun of the new morning.

All day, prayers were broadcast on television. An

imam sat on a carpet, swinging his body forward and back. In front of him a religious book lay open. He recited each verse in a lamenting voice.

That morning the *ulema* and the elders of the royal family selected a young brother of the dead king, the crown prince, as the new king. The transition was peaceful and the National Guard and the army returned to their barracks. There was no period of mourning.

They flew the King's body from his palace in the western hilly town to the capital, and took him to the ancient mosque in the city. After the prayers they took the late King in a hearse to the desert, to the area where his father and other dead family members were buried. The imams placed the body in the deep grave in the rocky, rugged desert, took the top covering sheet off and started filling the grave with rocky soil, and dust started to rise from the grave.

A deposed African dictator, who had been given political asylum in the country and was now living in luxury in a villa on the west coast, attended the funeral, laden with all kinds of medals that he had given himself. This obese dictator, who had challenged the British Commonwealth single-handedly, was so distraught, was wailing so loudly, looking at the television cameras and trying to jump into the King's grave. They held him back, although in his own country many would have obliged him by burying him alive. He was led away, swinging his tartan kilt and showing his disappointment by looking at the television cameras and shaking his head.

After a few weeks the new King went abroad for a summit with other Arab leaders. The new King had given all the government employees an extra month's pay. The whole country had great hopes for the new King's reign. Before his arrival back from the summit, the country got ready to welcome him. They decorated buildings, trees and streets with strings of coloured bulbs.

Sayeed asked Abdul Mubarak whether he could take little Leila to show her the decorations of the city. Abdul Mubarak brought Leila to the laboratory in the evening. She wore a pleated short red dress and her hair was braided, with red bows tied over her ears. She wore matching red shoes. Abdul Mubarak said that he would come to the laboratory to fetch Leila later that evening, and told Sayeed not to hurry back.

Leila came and sat in the chair next to Sayeed. She leaned back in the chair with her feet hanging just over the edge. Sayeed looked at her and stroked her hair and gave her a packet of chocolate. Leila laughed, put a piece in her mouth and started chewing with her cheek bulging.

Sayeed took a taxi from the hospital to the city centre. He walked the streets with Leila, watching the different light decorations. Leila was excited to see the city decorated with so many lights. There were thousands of people, going from street to street to see the displays.

People drove their vehicles blowing horns and flashing lights and waving their green national flags out of their windows. Some stood on top of moving cars and trucks, videoing the lights.

Sayeed stopped at the beginning of the main street of the city. The whole street was filled with a mass of people walking in both directions.

He lifted Leila up so that she could see the lights better.

'Uncle Sayeed, my friend said the new King is very rich and he owns the whole country.'

'Yes, Leila.'

'My friend said he is a very kind man.'

'He is a kind man, Leila.'

'Uncle Sayeed, the city is so beautiful.'

'Yes, Leila.'

'Uncle Sayeed?'

'Yes, Leila.'

'I wish my ummi had come with us to see these lights.'

'Yes, Leila.'

'She would have smiled and been very happy looking at the decorations.'

'Yes, Leila.'

'Uncle Sayeed?'

'Yes, Leila.'

'Do you think my ummi is lost in this big city and she cannot find her way back to me?'

'Perhaps, Leila, perhaps,' Sayeed said, with tears in his eyes.